MEN

OF

INFLUENCE

MEN

OF

INFLUENCE

*The Potential of the Priesthood
to Lift the World*

ROBERT L. MILLET

DESERET
BOOK

SALT LAKE CITY, UTAH

Library of Congress Cataloging-in-Publication Data

Millet, Robert L.
　　Men of influence : the potential of the priesthood to lift the world / Robert L. Millet.
　　　　p. cm.
　　Includes bibliographical references and index.
　　ISBN 978-1-60641-095-0 (hardbound : alk. paper)
　　1. Mormon men—Religious life.　2. Priesthood—Church of Jesus Christ of Latter-day Saints.　3. Christian life—Mormon authors.　4. Church of Jesus Christ of Latter-day Saints—Doctrines.　I. Title.
　　BX8659.M545 2009
　　248.8′42088289332—dc22　　　　　　　　　　　　　　　　2009001346

Printed in the United States of America
Publishers Printing, Salt Lake City, UT

10　9　8　7　6　5　4　3　2　1

Ye who are called to labor and minister for God,
Blest with the royal priesthood, appointed by his word
To preach among the nations the news of gospel grace,
And publish on the mountains salvation, truth, and peace:

Oh, let not vain ambition nor worldly glory stain
Your minds so pure and holy; acquit yourselves like men.
While lifting up your voices like trumpets long and loud,
Say to the slumb'ring nations: "Prepare to meet your God!"

Then cease from all light speeches, light-mindedness, and
    pride;
Pray always without ceasing and in the truth abide.
The Comforter will teach you, his richest blessings send.
Your Savior will be with you forever to the end.

Rich blessings there await you, and God will give you faith.
You shall be crowned with glory and triumph over death,
And soon you'll come to Zion, and, bearing each his sheaf,
No more shall taste of sorrow, but glorious crowns receive.

(Hymns, no. 321)

CONTENTS

Contents

PREFACE

THE PRIESTHOOD OF ALMIGHTY GOD is intended to do more than allow men to preside over and conduct meetings; oversee the ordinances of salvation; and confer, ordain, and set apart to offices and callings, as important and vital as these labors are. The priesthood is the very power of God, the power by which worlds came rolling into existence, the power by which the gospel is preached, the sick are healed, the dead are raised, and by which souls who have exercised a lively faith and hope in Jesus Christ are everlastingly redeemed and glorified. It is God's power. He has chosen in his mercy and wisdom to delegate it to worthy boys and men. That delegation allows us to act in the place and stead of our Savior, to strive to so live that we may speak what he would speak, act as he would act, and bless as he would bless. It is a divine investiture of authority. It is a sacred trust.

This book, a sequel to *Men of Valor,* is intended to point us as priesthood holders to the divine reservoir of power that has been conferred upon us and to the righteous and everlasting influence we can have in the world. Though it is to be used on this earth, the priesthood is beyond anything earthly. It is a heavenly endowment intended to lift and lighten, to soothe and strengthen, to benefit and bless. Just how great is this power? We may never know in this life, but by and through the unspeakable work of the Spirit we may occasionally be granted a fleeting glimpse of who our God is and what it is that makes him who he is. A significant part of his essence, as well as his energies, is his priesthood. It is to better understand the nature of that most unusual authority and the means by which those who are called to labor may become a more powerful influence in our homes, communities, and nation that this short work has been prepared. It is not intended to be comprehensive but concise. It is intended not to be scholarly but sustaining.

Let me say at the outset that this short work will speak occasionally of grand ideals and of powerful experiences, of the fruits of faith and of the infinite nature of God's divine power that is within our grasp. I write of these things not from a position of personal spiritual attainment but rather as one who has sought understanding on the matter and, more important, one who longs with all his heart that one day, these attainments, these grand spiritual experiences promised in holy writ, may be yours and mine on a more regular basis. For me, as with most of humankind, the ideal is yet to become an unblemished reality. But I believe in focusing on the ideal and hope that this work will motivate others, with me, to strive toward the realization of righteous and enduring influence.

As always, I am indebted to many people who have helped to shape my thinking, particularly my beloved priesthood leaders through the decades who have built my faith in priesthood power by demonstrating that power in their own lives. I am grateful for men of power who have chosen to stand on higher ground and to resist the pull toward popularity while denying themselves of the pollutions and perils of this world. I thank God for noble examples of Christlike kindness, gentle persuasion, yet powerful leadership as manifest in their words and deeds. In his great intercessory prayer, Jesus said: "And for [the disciples'] sakes I sanctify myself, that they also might be sanctified through the truth" (John 17:19). As Jesus, so many priesthood leaders have distanced themselves from defilement and, in the process, provided motivation and encouragement to those they were called to direct.

I am persuaded that today's holders of the priesthood are as faith-filled, as noble, as charitable, as hard-working, and as spiritually influential as any in times past. Knowing that it took the righteous Enoch 365 years to establish Zion in ancient times (D&C 107:49; Moses 7:67–68), and that we probably do not have that much time to do the same in this last dispensation, is to some extent a marvelous compliment to those called and ordained today to bear the Holy

Priesthood. I have great confidence in the men of the Church, largely because of what I have observed in so many of them. I know something of their hearts, a good bit about their souls, a great deal about their yearnings to be loving husbands and fathers, dependable priesthood representatives, responsible citizens, and influential servants of the Almighty.

I express appreciation to my friends at Deseret Book Company, especially Boyd Ware and Cory Maxwell, both of whom suggested that a second book written to men of the priesthood would be worthwhile and well accepted. I thank Suzanne Brady, my friend and my editor, whose keen insights into doctrine and the English language have blessed many writers, especially me. While I have sought to be in harmony with the standard works and the teachings of living apostles and prophets, I alone am responsible for the conclusions drawn from the evidence cited. This book is a private endeavor and not an official work of The Church of Jesus Christ of Latter-day Saints or Brigham Young University.

Introduction

CALLED TO LABOR

EVEN BEFORE MY PARENTS BECAME active Latter-day Saints, I wanted to hold the priesthood. When our family did go to church, once a month or so, I was deeply impressed by the dignity and sincerity of those men who took so seriously the call to labor. Because in those days we were a part of a very large district, the journey to district (stake) conference was quite a drive, and people in the various wards and branches often made a family vacation out of it. Some in our ward, however, were unable to attend because they could not afford the trip.

And so it was our practice, perhaps the result of a local decision, to hold sacrament meeting in our ward house for those who were unable to travel to New Orleans. I can remember, as though it were yesterday, Brother Charles Dixon conducting the meeting; preparing, blessing, and passing the sacrament; and delivering the sermon to a congregation made up mostly of older women and a few children. He loved what he was doing, and it showed. He represented his Lord and Savior—he knew it, and I felt it. He did so with great delight, and his enthusiasm for his calling was contagious. He had been called to serve. He had been asked by our bishop to oversee this meeting, to labor in the vineyard of the Almighty. Observing his service had a significant influence on me.

It is no accident that priesthood holders have been called to labor, that we have been commissioned to bear and magnify our various callings. Several years ago in a Book of Mormon class for returned missionaries one of the students asked: "Brother Millet, there's something I don't quite understand. What difference does it make that my patriarchal blessing tells me that I am of the tribe of Ephraim?"

I extended the question to the class. "Does anyone else have the same question?"

About fifty of the eighty students hesitantly raised their hands. I was a little startled, to be honest, but felt the question to be important and worthy of a thoughtful answer. I quickly and quietly asked the Lord for guidance and found myself saying, "The declaration of lineage within your patriarchal blessing is as much a statement about who and what you *were* in your first estate as it is a statement of who you are now and what you will yet do and become."

Similarly, those who hold priesthood authority in this life may be assured that they were ordained to the Holy Priesthood After the Order of the Son of God before they were ever born. More specifically, as Alma taught, they exercised exceedingly great faith in the Savior and in the Father's plan of redemption, the great plan of happiness, and were sent to earth on a redemptive mission: to hold the priesthood, exercise priesthood power, and thereby be a leavening influence in a world that was desperately in need of light and truth and goodness. Theirs was the call, before they breathed the breath of life, to help fulfill the Abrahamic promise that his posterity would truly bless the nations (Alma 13:1–5; Abraham 2:8–11).

As Joseph Smith the Prophet declared: "Every man who has a calling to minister to the inhabitants of the world was ordained to that very purpose in the Grand Council of heaven before this world was" (*Teachings*, 365). Elder Parley P. Pratt spoke of the foreordination or election of individuals "to certain offices, as written in the scriptures. In other words, certain individuals . . . were chosen by the Head to teach, instruct, edify, improve, govern, and minister truth and salvation to others, and to hold the delegated powers or keys of government in the several spheres of progressive being.

"These were not only chosen, but were set apart by a holy ordinance in the eternal worlds" (*Key to the Science of Theology*, 40).

In short, we were called to bear the priesthood a long, long time ago, and that call was merely renewed and reextended to us when we had the Aaronic Priesthood bestowed upon us and were ordained a deacon. We have been called and assigned to labor in the Lord's cause, to function under his direction and sacred guidance, and to work as faithful agents to carry out the will of our Principal (D&C 64:29). The marvel is that he trusts *us* to assist him in bringing to pass the immortality and eternal life of our brothers and sisters (Moses 1:39), and he relies upon *us* to gather and feed his sheep (John 21:16–17; D&C 29:7). We must each be true to that trust by faithfully standing in the offices to which we have been appointed (D&C 107:99–100) and by magnifying our callings (D&C 84:33).

We have been called to labor. There is no more noble task in this world than extending ourselves in service and striving to motivate, inspire, uplift, and influence others toward greater righteousness. God and Christ are in the business of saving souls, and holders of the priesthood are employed in the same business. Jesus was not a CEO in his kingdom, and the living prophet is not a CEO in the Church. Jesus was not a personnel manager, and the local bishop is not called to manage people; he is called to *lead* them. If there is joy in heaven over one sinner who repents (Luke 15:7), let me be the one who repents with all the energy of my soul and thereby brings joy and rejoicing to angels and to my Father and God. And let me be the instrument of peace—the one who honors his priesthood, ensures that there is no iniquity in the Church (D&C 20:54), and tenderly helps others to see the error of their ways and turn to our Lord and Savior for relief and renewal.

We have been called to labor, to take up our cross daily—

indeed, to be "soldiers of the Cross"—and to deny ourselves of all ungodliness and worldly lusts (Smith, *Gospel Doctrine*, 91; see JST Matthew 16:26; Luke 9:23; Moroni 10:32). Our labor, our work, like that of Hyrum Smith's, is to keep the commandments of God with all our might, mind, and strength (D&C 11:20). I have learned, by painful and sweet experience that keeping the commandments is not terribly difficult to do. Now don't get me wrong: I have made my share of mistakes and committed more than my share of sins. But what I mean is this—I believe it is not difficult to point ourselves toward eternal life, pursue that course consistently and fervently, and stay in the mainstream of the Church until we safely and faithfully die and are received happily into paradise. Being human we will slip up once in a while. We fail to follow through on our commitments every single time. And yet, from all that I have learned, the Lord is merciful and probably as much concerned with our direction as he is with our specific geography.

When my bishop or stake president asks me, "Brother Millet, are you keeping the commandments of God?" I don't suppose he is asking, "Brother Millet, are you doing your duty perfectly, keeping your mind totally clean and constantly involved with eternal things, never making a mistake, never taking a backward step, never pursuing even the slightest detour?"

Of course I'm not. A reasonable translation of the original question might be stated thus: "Brother Millet, are you headed in the right direction? Have you made the decision to follow the Lord and stand as his witness? Are you going in the commandment-keeping direction? Do you need to repent?"

Keeping the commandments is difficult only when we try to hold onto Babylon at the same time we seek to embrace the principles of Zion. As the Lord himself taught us so poignantly, we cannot simultaneously serve two masters (Matthew 6:24). Truly, as James declared, "a double minded man is unstable in all his ways" (James 1:8).

Here is a little secret that I believe too many who have been called to labor in the kingdom have not yet learned: one of the grand keys to success in this life and eternal reward in the life to come is to cultivate the gift and gifts of the Holy Ghost. In this sense, we may be compared to a fish who discovers water last. Sometimes without recognizing it, we are immersed in a dispensation of revelation, surrounded by light and truth and understanding and priesthood power, so immersed that we occasionally become indifferent or desensitized to the magnificent light within our reach. To be effective servants, holders of the priesthood of Almighty God should have a righteous obsession with cultivating the Spirit in their lives by maintaining a determined resolve to avoid places and situations and, yes, even people whose influence is degrading and spiritually deflating.

Enjoying the influence of the Spirit of the Lord is also paramount if we are to have our minds transformed and our beings conformed to the image of Christ (Romans 12:2; Galatians 4:19; Alma 5:14). Without the refining influence of the Holy Ghost we cannot come to know the mind and will of our Principal. And without the ongoing presence of the Spirit of the Lord, we cannot sustain the desire, the strength, and the spiritual stamina to do all that is expected of us as covenant representatives of the Mediator of the covenant. We must therefore pray for the Spirit. We must plead for it. We must live for it. The enjoyment of the Holy Spirit is inextricably linked to the enjoyment of power in the priesthood, the power to be a noble influence. When God the third, the witness or Testator, is operating in our lives, we know the love of God (Smith, *Teachings,* 190). "For this is the love of God, that we keep his commandments: and *his commandments are not grievous* [burdensome, oppressive]" (1 John 5:3; emphasis added).

When we are in tune we desire, more than ever, to be the best we can be. When we are inspired we long for sweet fellowship with God. When we have acquired a spiritual perspective we recognize the commandments not as impediments but as helps, aids, guidelines, and allies in our quest for "peace in this world, and eternal life in the world to come" (D&C 59:23).

It is also essential that we men of the priesthood know, and feel it in our bones, that we are spiritually begotten sons of an eternal Heavenly Father and, with Christ our Exemplar, heirs to all the Father has (D&C 84:38). It is also vital that each of us knows our place in the royal family as literal descendants of Abraham, Isaac, and Jacob; we are heirs to the promises God made to them, "the fathers" (D&C 2:2; see also 27:10).

Those who are called to labor are people of covenant. The covenants into which we enter in this life are mortal reminders of premortal promises. They remind us of our distant past and point us toward a glorious future. When our eyes are focused on covenants, our eyes are likewise single to the glory of God. Elder Boyd K. Packer highlighted the importance of being a covenant people:

"Several years ago I installed a stake president in England. . . . He had an unusual sense of direction. He was like a mariner with a sextant who took his bearings from the stars. I met with him each time he came to [general] conference and was impressed that he kept himself and his stake on course.

"Fortunately for me, when it was time for his release, I was assigned to reorganize the stake. It was then that I discovered what that sextant was and how he adjusted it to check his position and get a bearing for himself and for his members.

"He accepted his release, and said: 'I was happy to accept the call to serve as stake president, and I am equally happy to accept my release. I did not serve just because I was under *call*. I served because I am under *covenant*. And I can keep my covenants quite as well as a home teacher as I can serving as stake president.'

"This president understood the word *covenant*.

"While he was neither a scriptorian nor a gospel scholar, he somehow had learned that exaltation is achieved by keeping covenants, not by holding high position.

"The mariner gets his bearing from light coming from celestial bodies—the sun by day, the stars by night. That stake president did not need a mariner's sextant to set his course. In his mind there was a sextant infinitely more refined and precise than any mariner's instrument.

"The spiritual sextant, which each of us has, also functions on the principle of light from celestial sources. Set that sextant in your mind to the word *covenant* or the word *ordinance*. The light will come through. Then you can fix your position and set a true course in life" (*Ensign*, May 1987, 23–24).

The priesthood of Almighty God has been conferred upon us to enable us to bless others. It has also been bestowed to bless us, to empower us to become more and more like the One after whom this sacred authority is named.

"By learning of Him," President Thomas S. Monson taught, "by believing in Him, by following Him, there is the capacity to become like Him. The countenance can change; the heart can be softened; the step can be quickened; the outlook enhanced. Life becomes what it should become. Change is at times imperceptible, but it does take place" (*Ensign*, January 2003, 4).

Priesthood holders, the call to labor has been issued. We have received it. Now is the time to act. We have a world to save, a nation to strengthen, a community to beautify, a family to teach and uplift and bless. There are souls out there, precious in the sight of God (D&C 18:10–16), who need what we have to offer. Let's go to work!

PROCLAIMING GOSPEL GRACE

WE HAVE BEEN "BLEST WITH THE royal priesthood, appointed by his word / To preach among the nations the news of gospel grace, / And publish on the mountains salvation, truth, and peace" (*Hymns,* no. 321).

And as priesthood holders, we are under covenantal obligation "to stand as witnesses of God at all times and in all things, and in all places that [we] may be in, even until death" (Mosiah 18:9). We are called to bear witness that there is a God, that he is our Heavenly Father, the Father of the spirits of all men and women (Numbers 16:22; 27:16; Hebrews 12:9), that he has a body of flesh and bones as tangible as man's (D&C 130:22), and that we are created in his image and likeness. We are called to bear witness that our Father has a plan for the redemption and happiness of his children, a grand plan of salvation, and that there is purpose and meaning to all that we experience or undergo in this life.

We are commissioned to testify of the living reality of

Jesus of Nazareth—of his virgin birth, his divine Sonship, his matchless life, his timeless teachings, his atoning sacrifice, and his resurrection from the dead. We who have received a remission of sins through his cleansing blood and who have had the Spirit bear witness of the immortality of the soul are charged to share these truths with the world.

A testimony must be kept up to date, for we have been instructed to "live by every word that proceedeth forth from the mouth of God" (D&C 84:44; see also Matthew 4:4). In that spirit, we are similarly assigned to testify of the prophetic call of Joseph Smith Jr. and of the religious revolution he set in motion, which we know as the Restoration, for it is incumbent upon "every man who hath been warned to warn his neighbor" (D&C 88:81). That warning includes a declaration that doctrinal truths have been given from heaven as clarifying and restored gems for the faithful and that divine authority has been delivered by heavenly messengers through the laying on of hands (Smith, *Teachings,* 366). Accompanying that conviction is a witness that The Church of Jesus Christ of Latter-day Saints, as now constituted with prophets and apostles at its head, is the custodian of the fullness of the everlasting gospel, charged to prepare a people for the second coming of the Son of Man.

Priesthood holders are called to preach the gospel. Jesus himself commissioned us to go into all the world and make disciples of all nations (Matthew 28:19–20). That great commission was renewed in modern revelation: "Go ye into all the world, preach the gospel to every creature, *acting in the authority which I have given you,* baptizing in the name of the Father, and of the Son, and of the Holy Ghost" (D&C 68:8; emphasis added). Missionary work is a blessed burden that comes with Church membership, an assignment from the Lord that comes through being ordained to the priesthood. As member-missionaries we do not require special settings apart, for we have already been confirmed and ordained. We have the Spirit, and we have the power. What more do we need?

Perhaps some of us need a bit more courage and confidence. I shudder a bit when I think back on my full-time mission, when I routinely approached total strangers and boldly bore my testimony in Central Park; when I stood across the street from the New York Stock Exchange and delivered a sermon on the Apostasy and the Restoration to a crowd of curious onlookers; when I knocked without fear on the doors of the homes of hippies in Greenwich Village in 1968 and unashamedly spoke to them of sacred things; when my companion and I fearlessly accepted an invitation to address a group of Roman Catholic monks at a monastery and boldly told them our story. When I reflect on these things now, I marvel. How in the world did a shy kid from Louisiana dare mingle and mix with people far more knowledgeable and experienced in the sophisticated northeastern part of the country? The best answer is that I knew I had been called of God and that my message was true. The Spirit of the Lord had borne witness to my heart, and that assurance engendered courage and boldness.

To be sure, not every gospel conversation we have with those of other faiths will result in a convert baptism, but many will. Even chats that do not bear immediate fruit will have been worthwhile. People need to know that Latter-day Saints are not wild-eyed members of a strange cult, that we really do show up in public places and are not hiding out in enclaves or some vault in the mountains. Those not of our faith need to see that we are accessible and not just a weird and bizarre bunch. The only way they can know anything about us is through their interactions with us. And the more positive the interaction is, the more positive their impression of Mormonism will be. People will only ask us who we are, why we are, and what we believe when they perceive us as normal, nonthreatening, ordinary individuals who share their interests in peace, happiness, and family. It will also help if we smile.

"You are already wonderful missionaries," Elder Jeffrey R. Holland has assured us, "better than you think you are, and there is more where that comes from! The 12-hour-a-day, heavy-duty effort we'll leave to the full-time missionaries, but why should they have all the fun? We are entitled to a seat at the abundant table of testimony as well, and fortunately a place has been reserved there for each member of the Church. . . .

"Above all else we can live the gospel. Surely there is no

more powerful missionary message we can send to this world than the example of a loving and happy Latter-day Saint life. The manner and bearing, the smile and kindness of a faithful member of the Church brings a warmth and an outreach which no missionary tract or videotape can convey. People do not join the Church because of what they know. They join because of what they feel, what they see and want spiritually. Our spirit of testimony and happiness in that regard will come through to others if we let it" (*Ensign,* May 2001, 14).

During the time I was serving as director of the institute of religion near Florida State University, I was also pursuing my doctoral degree in religious studies. It was a terribly busy and hectic time as Shauna and I sought to juggle work, Church assignments, and education. I prayed incessantly for the energy to do it all, for the ability to express love and concern for my wife and children when we had limited time together. I prayed for the Lord to enlighten my mind and sharpen my intellect as I entered a world of study that was absolutely novel and even foreign to me. And because I was the first Latter-day Saint to be accepted into the religious studies program at FSU, I prayed to be the best I could be, to be a good student, to be an example of the believer, to make appropriate comments at the right time, and to know when it was best to speak out and when it was best to remain silent. I prayed, more specifically, for the opportunity to be able to share my testimony of the gospel and assist others—many of whom would go on to become ministers and priests—to come away from our five-year exchange with open and positive feelings toward the Church.

Those opportunities generally happened when I least expected them. On one occasion the students were told that a scholar visiting from Harvard would be speaking in the afternoon. It was there that I first met Professor Krister Stendahl, dean of the Harvard Divinity School and one of the most respected New Testament scholars in the country. His topic was Jesus and the Pharisees. Dr. Stendahl was a fascinating gentleman, one who clearly knew his subject extremely well. But it was a hot, miserable day. And his lecture was given in the afternoon, after lunch. And so as I looked around the room I noticed that about half of the students had drifted quietly into a blissful sleep.

At least until Dr. Stendahl said, "You know, there is a Gospel in which there are no Pharisees." A few sets of eyes opened and chins came off the chests. He then changed his statement to a question: "Did you know that in fact there is a Gospel in which there are no Pharisees?" People were looking around, wondering what in the world he was talking about or perhaps what apocryphal work he might have reference to. Then he explained: "Yes, it is in the Book of Mormon. In a section of the Book of Mormon known as Third Nephi, there is a Gospel, an American Gospel, in which there are no Pharisees."

I was absolutely stunned. As I looked around the room, I realized that a large proportion of the young people there were staring at me, the only Mormon in the crowd. Stendahl went on to speak at some length about the similarities and differences between the canonical Gospels and what Latter-day Saints call the Fifth Gospel. I spoke with him after his remarks and learned that only a year earlier he had spoken on the Book of Mormon at Brigham Young University at the invitation of Truman Madsen, who had hosted a conference, the proceedings of which were published as *Reflections on Mormonism: Judaeo-Christian Parallels.* As a result of his lecture, many of the students subsequently spoke with me about the Church and especially about the Book of Mormon.

Perhaps a year later I decided to go early to the seminar room where we held class on campus. I had some reading to catch up on, and so I arrived about an hour before starting time. I was only five minutes into my reading when the door opened and four of my fellow students entered.

"Hi, Bob. What are you doing here so early?" they asked.

I explained that I had come to do some reading, and they nodded. In a few minutes one young man, a Roman Catholic, said, "Bob, I know you need to get your work done, but could I ask you a favor? Would you be willing to take a few minutes and sketch out on the blackboard for us how the Mormons understand the purpose of life? I mean, what's life all about? What happens when we die? Stuff like that."

It was one of many times that I have felt the quiet whisperings of the Spirit to the effect that this scene was no accident, that he who knows all things had orchestrated the day and the time and had stirred the interest. Most of the hour was spent in wonderful, thoughtful conversation. It was a momentous missionary experience.

The Church of Jesus Christ of Latter-day Saints has grown in phenomenal fashion during its relatively brief history. In fact, the Church reached its first million members in 1947, the year I was born. At the end of 2007, the Church was the fourth largest Christian church in the United States with more than thirteen million members spread throughout the world. Impressive. But not an achievement worthy of boasting. We have miles and miles to go before we rest in the highest glory hereafter. And there is no way under the heavens that we will ever reach all the world and see our membership climb into the hundreds of millions, as prophesied, with a little more than fifty thousand full-time missionaries. Yes, of course the number of full-time ambassadors of the Lord will increase as demographics change and as a larger proportion of available young people serve missions, but that is not the answer to our problem.

President Monson, in his opening address to the October 2008 general conference, said, "There remain, however, areas of the world where our influence is limited and where we are not allowed to share the gospel freely. As did President Spencer W. Kimball over 32 years ago, I urge you to pray for the opening of those areas, that we might share with them the joy of the gospel. As we prayed then . . . , we saw miracles unfold as country after country . . . was opened. Such will transpire again as we pray with faith" (*Ensign,* November 2008, 6).

Listen to these words of a modern prophet, President Gordon B. Hinckley: "If the [missionaries] do it alone, they will knock on doors day after day and the harvest will be meager. Or as members we can assist them in finding and teaching investigators. . . .

"Brothers and sisters, all of you out in the wards and stakes and in the districts and branches, I invite you to become a vast army with enthusiasm for this work and a great overarching desire to . . . carry the gospel to every nation, kindred, tongue, and people" (*Ensign,* May 1999, 107, 110).

Clearly the answer lies with us, with every deacon, teacher, priest, elder, high priest, patriarch, seventy, and apostle. What we need is a change in perspective, an alteration in our outlook. How often do we hear well-meaning members of the Church pray, "We ask thee to bless our missionaries throughout the world. Lead them to the doors of the honest in heart." Such a prayer seeks to excuse us from joining in the labor. In 1976 Elder Bruce R. McConkie wisely observed that a prayer "places the responsibility for missionary work upon a handful of missionaries. How much better it would be if all the members of the Church assumed their full responsibility to do missionary work and said instead, 'We are so grateful for these . . . missionaries. *We want them to help us convert our contacts to the Church.*' Nobody helps the missionaries; rather, missionaries help all of us" (*Let Every Man*, 5; emphasis added).

When we pray for our missionaries, it would be well to add, "and bless us with the strength and the desire to help them." For we too have been called to labor, "to preach among the nations the news of gospel grace." Another way of putting it is to say that we have been called to "declare glad tidings of great joy," as the Savior explained to Thomas B. Marsh (D&C 31:3). We accept and endorse and seek to spread the good news that salvation is in Christ; that he is our Lord and Redeemer; that salvation comes only through his merits, mercy, and grace (2 Nephi 2:8; 31:19; Moroni 6:4). Salvation, or eternal life, is free (2 Nephi 2:4). It is the greatest of all the gifts of God (D&C 6:13; 14:7). In the words of Elder Jeffrey R. Holland: "Some gifts coming from the Atonement are universal, infinite, and unconditional. . . . Other aspects of Christ's atoning gift are conditional. They depend on one's diligence in keeping God's commandments. . . . Of course *neither the unconditional nor the conditional blessings of the Atonement are available except through the grace of Christ*. Obviously the unconditional blessings of the Atonement are unearned, but the conditional ones are not fully merited either. By living faithfully and keeping the commandments of God, one can receive additional privileges; but they are still given freely, not technically earned" (*Ensign*, March 2008, 35–36; emphasis added).

Certainly we teach Jesus Christ and him crucified

(1 Corinthians 2:2). He and the Atonement are at the foundation of our religion and constitute the very root of Christian doctrine, the only means by which other related doctrines have meaning and purpose (Smith, *Teachings,* 121; Packer, *Ensign,* May 1977, 56). But there is a value added to the message of the Restoration. It is not a value added to the Atonement of our Lord, for that supreme act is wholly sufficient, and we are "complete in him" (Colossians 2:10).

The value added to the message of the Restoration is that we declare Jesus Christ and him crucified, not only as set forth in the Bible but also as revealed through the instrumentality of a modern prophet, Joseph Smith. New revelation and additional scripture—given principally to bear witness of the Redeemer (1 Nephi 13:34-40)—has been delivered. Brother Joseph, as the head of the dispensation of the fullness of times, stands in our day as the preeminent prophetic revealer of Christ and the Father's plan of salvation.

The news of gospel grace is that the heavens have been opened. The Father and the Son appeared in a grove in upstate New York in the spring of 1820. Angels have been sent from the courts of glory to declare doctrine and confer priesthoods and keys. The fullness of the gospel is available to each honest seeker after truth. Apostles and prophets preside once again over the Lord's kingdom, and "the knowledge and power of God are expanding" and spreading throughout the earth (*Hymns,* no. 2). Ours is a day foreseen by the ancients, the time of the restitution of all things (Acts 3:21), the era when all the streams and rivers of past dispensations are flowing into the ocean of revealed truth.

As priesthood holders, we are a part of the beginnings of this marvelous work and a wonder (Isaiah 29:13–14), and the God of heaven will provide the necessary "proofs" to attract the seeker and lead the honest in heart to partake of the fruit of the tree of life. God is able to do his own work (2 Nephi 27:20), but thankfully he has commissioned and called us, the bearers of his holy priesthood, to assist him—to stand up, to speak out, to be unhesitant to share our pearl of great price, to be a powerful influence for good. "Look unto me in every thought," he implores, "doubt not, fear not" (D&C 6:36). Be assured, God is our partner, and in his strength we will not fail.

POINTS TO PONDER

1. Where would I be, what would I be, without the restored gospel in my life?

2. What specific differences have the Church and the gospel made in my daily life? In my family life? In my social life?

3. What things keep me from sharing our message of gospel grace more regularly? What can I begin to do now, today, to remove some of those obstacles?

4. How often do I pray that the Lord will provide opportunities for me to share with someone who urgently needs what I know and feel?

2

STIFLING VAIN AMBITION

IT IS SO OFTEN THE CASE THAT A virtue can, by a slight misuse or perversion, become a vice. So it is with ambition. We applaud those who are creative, who seek new and unusual ways to do their job more effectively. We teach our daughters to look carefully for spiritual strength, dependability, consistency, kindness, and, yes, ambition in young men they date and may choose to marry. I want my sons-in-law not only to lead out spiritually and provide a loving atmosphere for my daughters and grandchildren but to be industrious, hard working, to have goals in life, to be progressing toward something of worth in their profession or trade. I assume most fathers feel the same way. We recognize and honor those who are ambitious, who have a strong work ethic, and who know where they want to go in life. Indeed, people without ambition tend to wander, to hop from one attractive enterprise to another. They are unstable, bored, stagnant, and easily distracted. They have trouble focusing on a main idea and difficulty in moving down a planned pathway.

It is worth noting that though some of the dictionary definitions of the word *ambition* are positive and affirming, a surprising number are negative. For example, "an ardent (orig. inordinate) desire for distinction; . . . ostentatious; . . . display, pomp; . . . personal solicitation of honours; an aspiration *to be, to do*" (*New Shorter Oxford English Dictionary*, 64). We can thus gain some appreciation of why "vain ambition" is included in the sobering list of sins that prevent those who are called from being chosen. "Behold, there are many called, but few are chosen. And why are they not chosen? *Because their hearts are set so much upon the things of this world, and aspire to the honors of men,* that they do not learn this one lesson—

"That the rights of the priesthood are inseparably connected with the powers of heaven, and that the powers of heaven cannot be controlled nor handled only upon the principles of righteousness.

"That they may be conferred upon us, it is true; but when we undertake to cover our sins, or to gratify our pride, *our vain ambition,* or to exercise control or dominion or compulsion upon the souls of the children of men, in any degree of unrighteousness, behold, the heavens withdraw themselves; the Spirit of the Lord is grieved; and when it is withdrawn, Amen to the priesthood or the authority of that man" (D&C 121:34–37; emphasis added).

I'd like you to consider some of the implications of this

sobering warning, given through the Prophet Joseph Smith while a prisoner in Liberty Jail.

First, *many are called, but few are chosen*. We could look at this statement in a number of ways. President Harold B. Lee declared that many of us who exercised exceedingly great faith in the premortal realm and who were there foreordained to hold and exercise that same divine authority on earth do not qualify here to do so. They fail to qualify because, as Alma explained, they "reject the Spirit of God on account of the hardness of their hearts and blindness of their minds, while, if it had not been for this they might have had as great privilege as their brethren" (Alma 13:4). President Lee pointed out that even though we have our "agency here, there are many who were foreordained before the world was, to a greater state than they have prepared themselves for here. Even though they might have been among the noble and great, from among whom the Father declared he would make his chosen leaders, they may fail of that calling here in mortality" (*Ensign,* January 1974, 5). That is, they were called there but are not chosen here.

The Savior commanded the early Latter-day Saints to build a temple in Kirtland, Ohio. From his elevated perspective, the people of the covenant did not act upon that command with exactness or with the sense of urgency it deserved. Consequently the Lord observed that *"there are many who have been ordained among you, whom I have called but few of them are chosen. They who are not chosen have sinned a very grievous sin, in that they are walking in darkness at noon-day"* (D&C 95:5–6; emphasis added).

We walk in darkness at noon-day when we postpone obedience. We walk in darkness at noon-day when we choose to place other priorities higher than the highest ones. We walk in darkness at noon-day when we live beneath our spiritual privileges, when we have access to the mysteries of the kingdom of heaven and the very powers of godliness but choose instead to exist on borrowed light and are content with life as usual. Indeed, we walk in darkness when we obscure the light of heaven by distraction, preoccupation, and spiritual complacency.

We who are called to labor in the Lord's vineyard are summoned to embrace the sacred and shun the profane; to discern between primary and secondary causes; to live in a manner that the Holy Ghost is more than a distant acquaintance; to familiarize ourselves with holy writ to the point where our thoughts and vocabulary and speech are colored and perfumed by the words of life and where our actions are the actions of our divine Principal. We gradually, hour by hour and day by day, cultivate the Spirit of God and the powers of the priesthood as we learn to "walk in the light, as he [Christ] is in the light" (1 John 1:7), until on that great day of resurrection we will see him as he is. Why? Because we will have become like him (1 John 3:1–2).

The *vainly* ambitious in the kingdom of God "aspire to the honors of men" (D&C 121:35). Let us break this thought down. To begin with, there is nothing wrong with aspiring to greatness, aspiring to spirituality, aspiring to be the best we can be. There is surely no sin in seeking to be better, sharper, more proficient, more intelligent, more effective. In fact, we really ought to work smarter in the Church and kingdom of God. And, second, there is nothing wrong with receiving the honors of men. Many of our great Church leaders of the past have been acknowledged nationally and internationally for their gifts, talents, and contributions. Elder Ezra Taft Benson of the Quorum of the Twelve Apostles was appointed United States Secretary of Agriculture in the Eisenhower administration from 1952 to 1960. Elder Richard L. Evans of the Quorum of the Twelve served as president of Rotary International. President Thomas S. Monson has received some of the highest recognitions offered by the Boy Scouts of America for a life of dedication to this marvelous organization. And the same is true for many other members of the Church. Thousands of our youth serve as school or class officers; many of our women have been recognized as Mother(s) of the Year; and large numbers of our academic, political, military, and industrial leaders have become known and sought after, around the world, for their expertise. This is how it should be: the disciples of Christ, the Saints of the Most High, are called to be the salt of the earth and the light of the world, to make a difference because they are different, to allow their influence to be felt (Matthew 5:13–16; 3 Nephi 12:13–16).

Where we get into difficulty is not in aspiring, nor is it in receiving honors. It is *when we aspire to the honors* of men. That is, we cross the line of gospel propriety *when we seek* for the honors of others. Let's be realistic for a moment. Each of us wants to feel needed, to feel appreciated, to be told that our meager efforts make a difference and that we are genuinely valued. In short, we all would like to be counted as persons worthy of recognition and honor. But we must be patient enough to take the distant view, to recognize that not all wrongs are righted in this life, not all noble actions are acknowledged, and that not all hard work is rewarded. Some is, to be sure. As we mature in the things of the Spirit, however, we begin to find personal satisfaction in a job well done, a good deed rendered, a church calling magnified, even if those contributions are not publicly acknowledged. Ideally, we are content to know what we have done and to know that God knows it. We feel no need to have it broadcast far and wide. Indeed, to the extent that our meritorious actions are praised in public and people slap us on the back and drown us in their compliments, we have our reward (Matthew 6:2, 5; 3 Nephi 13:2, 5).

While it does not appear to be a significant problem, there are some within the household of faith who aspire to Church callings and assignments. This sister would really love to be the Relief Society president, and that brother would give anything to be called as bishop. In some cases, these desires are not all bad, because the individual would simply like to know that she or he is known by our Father in heaven, enjoys his favor, and, frankly, is worthy to be called to such an important responsibility. This may be what the apostle Paul had in mind in his counsel to Timothy: "This is a true saying, If a man desire the office of a bishop, he desireth a good work" (1 Timothy 3:1). (Or, as rendered in the Millet Revised Version, "If a man desireth the office of bishop, he is mentally unstable." I consider this to be prima facie evidence, irrefutable scriptural proof, that Paul never served as a bishop!)

On the other hand, if a man wants to be a bishop in order to have people think highly of him, his motives are impure. If a woman wants to be the Relief Society president in order to be in a position of authority and prominence, her desires are out of bounds. As President J. Reuben Clark Jr. stated so eloquently, "In the service of the Lord, it is not *where* you serve but *how.* In The Church of Jesus Christ of Latter-day Saints, one takes the place to which one is duly called, which place one neither seeks nor declines" (Conference Report, April 1951, 154; emphasis added).

The Prophet Joseph Smith "spoke of the disposition of many men to consider the lower offices in the Church dishonorable, and to look with jealous eyes upon the standing of others who are called to preside over them; that *it was the folly and nonsense of the human heart for a person to be aspiring to other stations than those to which they are appointed of God for them to occupy;* that it was better for individuals to magnify their respective calling, and wait patiently till God shall say to them, 'come up higher'" (*Teachings,* 223–24). Or, stated more concisely, "everyone should aspire only to magnify his own office and calling" (*Teachings,* 227).

President Dieter F. Uchtdorf spoke of those members of the Church who seek to hide, who search for a cave, and those members who seek to lead, who search for a crown. "Those who seek to lead may feel they are capable of doing more than what they are currently asked to do. . . .

"Brethren, when we stand before the Lord to be judged, will He look upon the positions we have held in the world or even in the Church? Do you suppose that titles we have had other than 'husband,' 'father,' or 'priesthood holder' will mean much to Him? Do you think He will care how packed our schedule was or how many important meetings we attended? Do you suppose that our success with filling our days with appointments will serve as an excuse for failure to spend time with our wife and family?

"The Lord judges so very differently from the way we do. He is pleased with the noble servant, not with the self-serving noble" (*Ensign,* November 2008, 54–55).

The warning is not simply against ambition but against *vain* ambition. Something is vain when it is empty, shallow, meaningless in the eternal scheme of things. We have been called to labor. We have been selected to make choices, to set priorities, to see to it that we value some things more than others. "Lay not up for yourselves treasures upon earth,"

Jesus counseled, "where moth and rust doth corrupt, and where thieves break through and steal: but lay up for yourselves treasures in heaven, where neither moth nor rust doth corrupt, and where thieves do not break through nor steal. For *where your treasure is, there will your heart be also*" (Matthew 6:19–21; emphasis added). There are men throughout the world who labor long hours in making a living. Some spend the greater part of the day adding to their pile of surplus, expanding upon the affluence they have already attained. Others build houses that more closely approximate castles, residences that almost resemble cathedrals.

The Lord's commission to each of us is to "Come, my brethren, every one that thirsteth, come ye to the waters; and he that hath no money, come buy and eat; yea, come buy wine and milk without money and without price." Now note this pressing passage: "Wherefore, *do not spend money for that which is of no worth, nor your labor for that which cannot satisfy*" (2 Nephi 9:50–51; compare Isaiah 55:1–2; emphasis added). Every family, to the extent that it can do so, likes to enjoy the little comforts, luxuries, and niceties that make life pleasurable, but we must, at the same time, take seriously the words of our Lord: "Take heed, and beware of covetousness: for a man's life consisteth not in the abundance of the things which he possesseth" (Luke 12:15). In other words, the cute and coy aphorism that "He who dies with the most toys wins" is not really true, especially in regard to eternal matters. As Elder Lance B. Wickman taught: "This life is not so much a time for getting and accumulating as it is a time for giving and becoming" (*Ensign,* May 2008, 105).

It is tragic to witness how often men who would never consider being unfaithful to their wives are less than faithful in their priesthood responsibilities; those who would not think twice about whether to pursue the sexual pollutions of our day who yield instead to the persuasions of pleasurable living and spend most of their time in the lap of luxury; and those who are in constant search for some new toy, some new investment, some new avenue to even greater prosperity, whose search of the scriptures and the sermons of living apostles and prophets is limited to what is discussed in church on the Sabbath.

I say all of this to remind each of us why we came to earth in the first place, how urgently our wives and children and friends and neighbors need our righteous influence and our service, and where exactly peace and contentment are ultimately to be found. "We have been entrusted to bear the priesthood and to act in the name of God," President Thomas S. Monson testified. "We are the recipients of a sacred trust. Much is expected of us. We who hold the priesthood of God and honor it are among those who have been reserved for this special period in history" (*Ensign,* November 2007, 59).

Being foreordained is all about coming to the earth at a specific time, through a chosen lineage, to a designated place—all as a result of the faith we exercised in our premortal existence. We were true and faithful there and then. We have been foreordained to greatness, but we must be reminded frequently that "to do well those things which God ordained to be the common lot of all mankind, is the truest greatness" (Smith, *Gospel Doctrine*, 285).

Notice what the Master stated in regard to William W. Phelps in 1831: "And also let my servant William W. Phelps stand in the office to which I have appointed him, and receive his inheritance in the land [Missouri]; and also *he hath need to repent,* for I, the Lord, am not well pleased with him, for *he seeketh to excel,* and he is not sufficiently meek before me" (D&C 58:40–41; emphasis added). What an odd expression. Shouldn't we seek to excel? Shouldn't those called to labor, the men of the priesthood, excel? Doesn't the Father expect us to live an excellent life, to pattern ours after his Most Excellent Son? Certainly we should do the work of the Lord excellently. We should have an excellent record of home teaching, an outward indication that we are meeting regularly with our assigned families, strengthening our bonds of friendship, and nurturing them by the good word of God (Moroni 6:4). Certainly we should seek to hold excellent, as opposed to shoddy, family prayers, family scripture readings, and family home evenings. Certainly we should be excellent in our attendance at church meetings, a regular, active, practicing, and involved member of the body of Christ. And so forth.

What we do not want to do, however—as W. W. Phelps was chastened for doing—is to "seek to excel," that is, to do things to be considered excellent, to gain the applause of fickle observers. "It is natural to assume," wrote Elder Bruce C. Hafen, "that when we don't appear to be doing 'excellently' the perfection process is not working. But the exact opposite may be true. Our moments of greatest stress and difficulty are often the times when the refiner's fire is doing its most purifying work. . . .

"I am addressing primarily a need for perspective," Elder Hafen continued. "I do not mean to diminish the value of serious commitments to personal achievement and responsibility. . . . But *the striving must be to find out God and to accept fully the experiences he knows will enlarge our souls.* The trouble with modern pursuits of excellence is that they can become a striving to please other people, or at least to impress them or to seek their approval. A desire for such approval is not all bad, especially among Church members, who generally reserve their approval for accomplishments having positive value. But *other people are not finally our judge,* and making too much of either the affirmative or the adverse judgments of others can actually undermine our relationship with God and our development of sound values" (*Broken Heart,* 97–99; emphasis added).

In this regard, it is well to remember the warning given by President Joseph F. Smith, who declared the three great dangers that "threaten the Church within" are false educational ideas, sexual impurity, and the flattery of prominent men in the world (*Gospel Doctrine,* 313).

Our Lord and Redeemer taught a deeply profound lesson in few words: "I receive not honour from men" (John 5:41). Jesus was sent to earth to restore the gospel in its fulness, to teach the principles of salvation, to confer priesthoods and keys, and to offer immortality and eternal life to as many as would receive them. One imagines he wants desperately for his message to be adopted, for people to come unto him and find rest to their souls through remission of sins. But he did not court favor and was no respecter of persons (Acts 10:34). With all the light and knowledge and power at his disposal, he did not do things to make a good impression; he did not manage appearances, so that the Jews or the Gentiles would be wowed by his presence or his precepts. He was the Way, and he pointed the way. He was the Truth, and he taught the truth. He was the Life, and he offered the abundant life (John 14:6; 10:10). He "went about doing good" (Acts 10:38), but he did not put on airs. He served his fellow beings on earth, but he did so without fanfare. He lived a life in which he was constantly inconvenienced, but he never boasted of it. He was who he was, and he thereby stands as our Model and our Prototype. His ambition was sublime, the grandest and most profound of all ambitions, namely, to save every living soul.

POINTS TO PONDER

1. What really matters the most to me in this life? In eternity? Would my wife know that to be the case? Would my children? Would my business associates?

2. What are some activities or pursuits that catch my fancy that are nice but not necessary, lovely but not lasting?

3. Are my priorities in order? At some future day will I awaken to a whole new way of seeing things, namely, as the Lord sees them?

4. As a holder of the holy priesthood, do I have things in my life that the Son of God does not approve of? What actions or attitudes does he now beckon me to jettison?

MINDING OUR MINDS

WE WHO ARE CALLED TO LABOR ARE summoned to a divine service, a sacred duty where we are enjoined, "let not vain ambition nor worldly glory stain / Your minds so pure and holy;
acquit yourselves like men" (*Hymns,* no. 321). We will enjoy
power in the priesthood and be a worthy influence only to
the extent that we learn to "mind our minds," to attend to
what goes into our thinking and how it affects what we reflect on, feel, and do. The famous interview between James
Dobson, then president of Focus on the Family, and Ted
Bundy, the serial killer who may have been responsible for the
vicious murders of over a hundred women, affirmed an obvious truth: what we think about determines what we do.
Bundy stated to Dr. Dobson that his destructive path began
with his obsession with pornography. Sexually perverse and
warped thinking led eventually to violent and destructive behavior, until he was caught in the snare and bound with
the chains of hell. And what was the result? Lives wasted,

families devastated, and futures foreclosed because one man never learned to guard his mind.

There are plenty of offhand remarks, titillating advertisements, and off-color jokes all about us, things over which we have little or no control; the last thing in the world we need to do is to add to the array of filthiness and purposely bring additional sources of decay into our minds. Foolish indeed is the man who knowingly chooses to spend his time endlessly watching inane TV sitcoms or questionable movies, indulging in coarse or brutal behavior, listening to harsh or unclean music, absorbing magazine content that is foul, or becoming glued to the Internet—any and all of which corrupt the mind and soil the soul. To employ an analogy, we don't need to plant weeds—they grow up just fine by themselves!

Thoughts are seeds of action. Some years ago President Dallin H. Oaks explained to Brigham Young University students: "We are surrounded by the promotional literature of illicit sexual relations on the printed page and on the screen. For your own good, avoid it. Pornographic or erotic stories are worse than filthy or polluted food. The body has defenses to rid itself of unwholesome food, but the brain won't vomit back filth. Once recorded it will always remain subject to recall, flashing its perverted images across your mind, and drawing you away from the wholesome things in life" (in Tanner, *Ensign*, January 1974, 7-8).

We must *guard* our minds, defend that portion of the battlefront that is ours to protect, and see to it that the enemy of our salvation is not permitted incursions into friendly territory. We must also *discipline* our minds. It makes little sense that a man would spend hours running, walking strenuously, working out with weights regularly, and eating healthy foods, only to leave his mind in flabby condition—untrained, untutored, undisciplined, and consequently unprotected. Mental discipline may entail looking the other way, reading good literature and filling our minds with worthy insights, memorizing great sayings and especially scriptural passages, listening to inspirational music or general conference addresses as we drive, and pleading that God Almighty will in general help us to stand bravely above the rising tide of immorality, secularism, and cynicism.

"Finally, brethren, whatsoever things are true, whatsoever things are honest, whatsoever things are just, whatsoever things are pure, whatsoever things are lovely, whatsoever things are of good report; if there be any virtue, and if there be any praise, THINK ON THESE THINGS" (Philippians 4:8; emphasis added). President Thomas S. Monson bore witness to the men of the priesthood that "the face of sin today often wears the face of tolerance. Do not be deceived; behind that façade is heartache, unhappiness, and pain. You know what is right and what is wrong, and no disguise, however appealing, can change that. The character of transgression remains the same" (*Ensign,* May 2008, 65).

"Preach unto [the people] repentance," Alma counseled, "and faith on the Lord Jesus Christ; teach them to humble themselves and to be meek and lowly in heart; *teach them to withstand every temptation of the devil, with their faith on the Lord Jesus Christ"* (Alma 37:33; emphasis added). Alma's words provide a clear and straightforward but profoundly important formula for engaging and overcoming Satan.

First, we need to repent of our sins, to cleanse our minds and our whole souls of vice and iniquity. When we harbor sin, we attract other sin. When we cover and hide the sinful behavior of our past, our duplicity prevents us from feeling and internalizing the powers of the Holy Ghost. Purity precedes power. Remission of sins brings strength and spiritual stamina. When we are no longer holding onto our transgressions, we are able to grasp the shield of faith and the sword of the Spirit (D&C 27:17–18) and fight manfully for the cause of righteousness. Cleansed and spiritually endowed, we can be a force for good and a noble influence.

Second, we must humble ourselves and be meek and lowly in heart. Humility is, of course, one of the most misunderstood of all gifts and divine attributes. It is not a sign of weakness, of ignorance, or of shyness. One who cowers in the corner and lets others do the talking is not necessarily humble. On the other hand, one who is filled with certitude, who is bold and fearless in declaring the truths of salvation, is not necessarily lacking humility. Humility is all about recognition and resolve—we recognize our human weakness and our need for deliverance and strength beyond our own. We demonstrate humility when we gladly acknowledge the hand of the

Lord and where the real power comes from and resolve to draw upon it. Humility is all about seeing things as they really are—who I am and who God is. King Benjamin taught that recognizing God's greatness and my own nothingness without his assistance—that is, living humbly—is one of the grand keys to retaining a remission of sins (Mosiah 4:11–12).

Meekness is certainly a first cousin to humility, but they are slightly different virtues and states of mind. One is meek who exercises poise under provocation, demonstrates emotional control, displays pious gentleness in nature, and is tame and mild-mannered. The Torah teaches that "the man Moses was very meek, above all the men which were upon the face of the earth" (Numbers 12:3). Jesus described himself as "meek and lowly in heart" (Matthew 11:29). Consequently, "none is acceptable before God, save the meek and lowly in heart" (Moroni 7:44). In short, the meek shall inherit the celestialized earth (Matthew 5:5; 3 Nephi 12:5). "In a world too preoccupied with winning through intimidation and seeking to be number one," President Howard W. Hunter pointed out, "no large crowd of folk is standing in line to buy books that call for mere meekness. But *the meek shall inherit the earth, a pretty impressive corporate takeover—and done without intimidation!* Sooner or later, and we pray sooner *than* later, everyone will acknowledge that Christ's way is not only the right way, but ultimately the *only* way to hope and joy. Every knee shall bow and every tongue will confess that *gentleness is better than brutality, that kindness is greater than coercion, that the soft voice turneth away wrath.* In the end, and sooner than that whenever possible, we must be more like him" (*Ensign,* May 1993, 64–65; emphasis added).

The climax of Alma's exhortation to Helaman is to "withstand every temptation of the devil, with [your] faith on the Lord Jesus Christ" (Alma 37:33). The question is, How does my faith in Christ help me to overcome temptation, especially to dismiss thoughts that have no place in the mind of one interested in spiritual things? To have faith in Christ is to have total trust, complete confidence, and a ready reliance on him and in his redeeming powers. It is to believe him when he says that he is the Son of God. It is to accept the prophetic word that peace and joy and salvation, here and hereafter, come in and through his holy name and in no other way (Acts 4:12; Mosiah 3:17). It is to trust him, his prophets, and the scriptures sufficiently that we "come boldly unto the throne of grace, that we may obtain mercy, and find grace to help in time of need" (Hebrews 4:16). Enoch likewise rejoiced in the fact that the Father had "made me, and given unto me a right to thy throne, and not of myself, but through thine own grace" (Moses 7:59).

That's the theology. What's the religion? What's the practicality? It is that my faith in Christ allows me to maintain perspective, to keep the big picture, the distant view. For example, if I knew that I needed a thousand dollars to pay a bill within three months, I would do well to begin saving and start avoiding unnecessary purchases. I would eat out less often and plan my driving activities so as to maximize the gasoline in the car. The day when the payment will come due will arrive sooner than I think, and so I do all I can in the remaining time to prepare. In the same way, in a not too distant future (indeed, I am now much closer to the crypt than to the cradle) I will pass through the veil of death and be required to answer for who I am and what I have become. I cannot picture the Lord Jesus or one of his designated servants going through a type of spiritual laundry list of all the things I have done right as compared with all the things I have done wrong. I can picture, however, an assessment of my character, an evaluation of the depth of my Christianity as reflected in the way I have behaved and in the manner in which I have come to worship God and serve his children.

That's the distant view. With that view in mind, it should matter very much to me how I spend my time (especially my leisure time), what I think about (especially when I am not required to think), and what I choose to take in and filter out of my brain. When the time comes, I want to be able to look my Lord in the eyes and feel comfortable. I do not want to be nervous, ill at ease, or frightened. I do not want to feel out of place. Rather, I want to feel welcome. Settled. Home at last. Peaceful. And loved. To do so, I must in this life be striving to avoid whatever would pollute or dilute or stain or scar or distract. I must be striving—and striving it is, for no one of us will pass through the veil in perfect form—to be clean from the sins of this generation, to be free from the barnacles and burdens that sap our strength and weaken our resolve.

My wife, Shauna, and I have a few things in common: we both enjoy reading, watching baseball and the Olympics, and playing with grandchildren. We also love, absolutely love, coconut cream pie. But Shauna is disciplined, whereas I am not. I confess that if coconut cream pie were placed before me as a dessert for three meals a day, I would eat it. I know that's not healthy, not wise, not even sane, but I think it has something to do with a chemical imbalance in my brain. I have no satiation mechanism when it comes to eating this, my favorite pie. By that I mean there's nothing within me that calmly or even savagely cries out, "Bob, that's enough. You can stop now. Four slices of pie is plenty."

When Shauna and I go out to dinner, especially if we're in just the right restaurant, I will say toward the end of the meal, "Sweetheart, shall we have some coconut pie?" She will smile, sigh, and then say, "No, you go ahead. I'm fine."

It's really disgusting. Do you know what I mean?

A few times I have argued with her about her discipline. "But you love coconut cream, don't you?"

She will respond calmly, "You know I do, but I don't need any now."

I come back with, "I know you don't *need* it. Nobody *needs* it. But I *want* it. Don't you?"

And then she brings our conversation to an end with, "Yes, I want it, but I want some things more. I want to avoid obesity, to be able to wear my clothes, to have good health, and to watch my grandkids grow up. Besides, I know that in thirty minutes I'll regret having eaten the pie. It's just not worth the five minutes of enjoyment."

I know Shauna is right. Lots of things would be nice, but some things are gratifying, inspiring, uplifting, and fulfilling. Present pleasure is nice, but the joys of overcoming, the unspeakable privilege of being able to look my family members in the eye, knowing that I have sought to be as clean and virtuous as I can—these more meaningful rewards come when we take the distant view, when we see the truth, things as they really are and as they really will be (Jacob 4:13; D&C 93:24), and when we act accordingly.

I remember walking from the institute of religion building to the Florida State University campus scores of times. This was a pleasant walk, filled much of the year with gorgeous flowers and large, beautiful oak trees. Unfortunately, as the spring of the year began to roll around, the clothing styles began to change. It was extremely difficult for the next several months to look up without seeing some lovely young woman scantily clad in that warm, humid climate. I applied Elder Boyd K. Packer's counsel on scores of occasions—that is, I sang most of the hymns in the hymnbook to myself in order to keep my thoughts out of forbidden territory and my mind and heart on safe and solid ground (*Ensign,* January 1974, 25). In fact, I spent a great deal of time looking at the ground or looking over people's heads or searching for less traveled routes to class.

To mind my mind is to *clear* my mind, to rid it of anger, jealousy, resentment, fear, feelings of inadequacy, inappropriate desires. It is to pray constantly that our Heavenly Father will, through the atoning blood of his Son and by the power of his Holy Spirit, wash and cleanse my thoughts and my feelings, empower me to think what I ought to think and feel what I ought to feel. Personal mental discipline is a necessary ingredient, but it is not sufficient. Grit and willpower may help, but they will not solve the problem. What we need is strength beyond our own, power above and beyond what any mortal could generate. We need God's grace—his unearned divine assistance, his unmerited divine favor, his enabling power—to successfully run the race of life and one day find ourselves at the proper finish line. We simply need help. We cannot "handle it." No one can handle it alone. We need good friends. We need positive influences in order to become a positive influence. We most definitely need the holy scriptures and the words of the prophets on our minds throughout the day. In speaking of his divine word, the Savior instructed: *"Treasure these things up in your hearts, and let the solemnities of eternity rest upon your minds"* (D&C 43:34; emphasis added).

Keeping our thoughts clean and our minds pure is a lifetime pursuit. Elder B. H. Roberts insightfully taught: *"There is an absolute necessity for some additional sanctifying grace that will strengthen the poor human nature, not only to enable it to resist temptation, but also to root out from the heart concupiscence—the blind tendency or inclination to evil.* The heart must be purified, every passion, every propensity made submissive to the will, and the will of man brought into subjection to the will of God.

"Man's natural powers are unequal to this task; so, I believe, all will testify who have made the experiment. Mankind stand in some need of a strength superior to any they possess of themselves, to accomplish this work of rendering pure our fallen nature. Such strength, such power, such a sanctifying grace is conferred on man in being born of the Spirit—in receiving the Holy Ghost. Such, in the main, is its office, its work" (*Man's Relationship to Deity*, 170; emphasis added).

Much of the time the Holy Ghost works quietly and imperceptibly upon the hearts and minds of the children of God, rubbing off a corner here and refining an edge there. Zion is established "in process of time" (Moses 7:21), and, with but few exceptions, men and women become pure and holy in the same manner. There are very few instant Saints. Individuals who are earnestly striving to keep the commandments and are in the line of their duty may not even notice how or in what manner they are changing; it is often others who most readily notice the change. We may begin to develop a deeper appreciation for quiet moments and come to treasure silence. We may begin to develop a reverence for life and a revulsion for violence. We may experience a heightened sensitivity to right and wrong—we simply find ourselves unable to feel good about doing some things we used to do. We may find our hearts reaching out to those who mourn, our feet rushing to assist those who are in need, our voices eager to express thanks and gratitude to those who serve us. And so on. "There is no friendship more valuable than your own clear conscience," President Monson declared, "your own moral cleanliness—and what a glorious feeling it is to know that you stand in your appointed place clean and with the confidence that you are worthy to do so" (*Ensign,* May 2008, 65).

Finally, I suggest, once again, that a vital key to minding our minds takes the form of *making up our minds,* deciding now, unquestionably, before it is too late, that we will do things the Lord's way. Any and all efforts to avoid being *conformed* to this world but rather seeking to have our minds *transformed* (Romans 12:1–2) is the spiritually safe and secure course to follow. In this way, and in this way only, we gain "the mind of Christ" (1 Corinthians 2:16) and are on the path of emulation of the great Prototype of all saved beings (Smith, *Lectures on Faith,* 7:9). That emulation is the highest form of worship.

POINTS TO PONDER

1. What do I think about when I don't have to think?

2. What can I add to my mental diet that would chase away darkness and bring a greater measure of light?

3. How often do I take the time to commit to memory scriptural passages or noble sayings in an effort to elevate my thoughts?

4. What would Jesus think if he were to read my mind?

ACQUIT YOURSELVES LIKE MEN

WHEN WE READ IN THE NEWSPAPER that so and so was acquitted of the crime for which he was arrested, we understand that the charges were dropped, the evidence against him was not felt to be sufficient for a conviction, and he has been declared innocent of the crime and set free. Nothing inside the acquitted man actually changed when the verdict of "not guilty" was rendered by the jury, but what changed was his *standing* before the law, his legal *status* before the people of the city and state. He was no longer "the accused." As far as the law is concerned, he is a *just* man.

Priesthood is the power and authority of God, delegated to man on earth, to act in all things pertaining to the salvation of the human family. Ours is a mission of blessing, an assignment to assist, a duty to make our little corner of the world a better place. The world, spiraling downward toward Sodom and Gomorrah, is in desperate need of men of purpose—men who know who they are, whose they are, and why they have been sent to the earth at this time. The world is in a crisis mode in its need for men of righteous influence.

When a man honors his priesthood and lives in a manner to allow God to work through him, he becomes a Christ figure, a true Christian, an ambassador of his divine Principal. Similar to his Exemplar, he is on a mission of redemption, a journey that will take him wherever God leads him. People listen when he speaks. He is more wise than witty, more character-filled than cute. There is substance to him; his waters run deep. He is a man, a real man, a priesthood man, a man of Christ.

As priesthood holders we are instructed in the hymn to see to it that our minds are pure and holy, to "acquit yourselves like men" (*Hymns,* no. 321). As stated earlier, one way to *acquit* ourselves is to be accounted not as "not guilty" but rather as "innocent." In that sense, we are called to become as a little child, for the revelations attest that they are innocent, or holy (D&C 74:7; 93:38).

Some six months before his crucifixion, Jesus was asked by his disciples: "Who is the greatest in the kingdom of heaven?" In answer, He "called a little child unto him, and set him in the midst of them, and said, verily I say unto you, *except ye be converted, and become as little children, ye shall not enter into the kingdom of heaven.* Whosoever therefore shall humble himself as this little child, the same is greatest in the kingdom of heaven" (Matthew 18:1–4; emphasis added; compare Luke 18:17.) Here we find that becoming as a little child is related to being *converted*. Becoming as a little child represents a turnaround, an alteration of behavior and attitude, a matter of "cross[ing] yourself" (Alma 39:9), of going at cross purposes to the natural man and moving toward God and godliness. The Lord does not call upon us to be childish but rather to be childlike. Though there are exceptions, especially in children who have met with tragic abuse or with conditions that might flaw their pure perceptions of life, a little child is:

Dependent. Children are dependent on their parents or other significant persons in their lives. They cannot live without help, and at some level they know it. They look to others for support and sustenance.

Submissive. Most young children readily admit and acknowledge that they are under the care and keeping of others. They look to the leadership of parents or loved ones and learn to abide by the standards of the family or of society.

Trusting. There is something very sobering about having a little one look into your eyes with trust and loyalty and an eagerness to please. Unless they are taught by the perverse to do otherwise, children are extremely trusting.

Humble. Most children are eager to learn, eager to be taught. They know, for the most part, what they don't know, and they want to change that. Their inquisitiveness is unaffected by pride and fear that others will think them deficient or inadequate for asking questions.

Patient and persistent. Children generally can sit and watch and listen to the simplest things for hours. They can wait almost indefinitely for an answer or for a solution to a problem.

Delighted by simple pleasures. Parents have sensed with some frustration at Christmastime that their little ones are just as happy to play with the cardboard boxes as they are to play with the expensive toys that came in those boxes.

Alive to life about them. What a refreshing and lifting pleasure it is to watch a child in a meadow or in a forest or on a street corner as he or she attempts with childlike zeal to take everything in. Children literally and metaphorically love to take time to smell the roses.

Not caught up with life's stresses and strains. They do not yield to life's pressures, the anxieties associated with planning and over-planning for tomorrow. They celebrate the present.

Quick to forgive and forget. Many a parent is heartsick for being impatient or overreactive to a child's behavior, only to find that within moments all is forgotten and forgiven from the child's point of view.

Pure. Above and beyond all that we have listed above, children are pure and innocent. Why are they pure? The man on the street might answer: "Children are pure because they are just that way by nature. They are innately good." But the scriptures teach otherwise. An angel taught Benjamin that "even if it were possible that little children could sin they could not be saved," if there were no Atonement; "but I say unto you they are blessed; for behold, *as in Adam, or by nature, they fall, even so the blood of Christ atoneth for their sins*" (Mosiah

3:16; emphasis added). Children are pure because our Master has decreed them so, as an unconditional benefit of his Atonement. "Little children are holy, being sanctified through the atonement of Jesus Christ; and this is what the scriptures mean" (D&C 74:7). God has instructed us that "little children are redeemed from the foundation of the world through mine Only Begotten" (D&C 29:46).

Truly the "poor in spirit," those who recognize their own spiritual bankruptcy and who then come unto Christ—these are they who inherit the kingdom of heaven (3 Nephi 12:3). All of us—every man, woman, and child—need the Lord. We need him desperately. We are eternally indebted and eternally dependent (Mosiah 2:19-24). Without God, without Christ, we are less than the dust of the earth (Mosiah 2:25; 4:2; Helaman 12:7-8). And the sooner we internalize that mighty truth, the sooner we begin to make progress toward life eternal. One of the transcendent ironies in the gospel plan is that the sincere and heartfelt recognition and acknowledgment of weakness and need open the channel for immeasurable strength and power—the Lord's power.

"And Jesus said, For judgment I am come into this world, that they which see not might see; and that they which see might be made blind. And some of the Pharisees which were with him heard these words, and said unto him, Are we blind also? Jesus said unto them, If ye were blind, ye should have no sin: but now ye say, We see; therefore your sin remaineth" (John 9:39-41). C. S. Lewis observed: "In God you come up against something which is in every respect immeasurably superior to yourself. Unless you know God as that—and, therefore, know yourself as nothing in comparison—you do not know God at all. As long as you are proud you cannot know God. A proud man is always looking down on things and people: and, of course, as long as you are looking down, you cannot see something that is above you" (*Mere Christianity*, 111).

A man of the priesthood, a just man, is one who has sought to humble himself before God, has sought to become as a little child, to become a child in Christ. "Contrition is costly," President Howard W. Hunter pointed out, "it costs us our pride and our insensitivity, but it especially costs us our sins" (*Joy*, 9). A man of the priesthood has begun to take his cues from within and from God rather than being driven and wafted about by the whims and taunts of a fallen world. "Wherefore, I beseech of you, brethren," Mormon declared, "that ye should search diligently in the light of Christ that ye may know good from evil; and if ye will lay hold upon every good thing, and condemn it not, ye certainly will be a child of Christ" (Moroni 7:19).

The Prophet Joseph Smith testified that "the Son of God came into the world to redeem it from the fall. But except a man be born again, he cannot see the kingdom of God. This eternal truth settles the question of all men's religion. A man may be saved, after the judgment, in the terrestrial kingdom, or in the telestial kingdom, but he can never see the celestial kingdom of God . . . unless he becomes as a little child, and is taught by the Spirit of God" (*Teachings,* 12). Ironic, isn't it? We become a real man, a priesthood man, by learning first to become as a little child. We acquit ourselves as men, to begin with, by repenting and allowing the Atonement to remit our sins and for the Spirit to affirm that we are "not guilty." We are innocent.

A second meaning of *acquit* is to discharge the duties or responsibilities of an office, to perform a labor, to accomplish a task. We begin by learning what we are to do through a careful and prayerful search of the scriptures and handbooks of the Church. I remember when I was first called to serve as bishop in Tallahassee, Florida, in 1978. My mom and dad drove over from Louisiana to attend the sacrament meeting where I was sustained and the setting apart afterwards. President Richard Chapple spoke briefly to me and my family, offered wise counsel, and, then, with his two counselors, laid his hands upon my head. He ordained me a bishop, set me apart as bishop of the Tallahassee First Ward, and then pronounced a compelling and sublime blessing. After "Amen" was said and handshakes and hugs were finished, we walked to the car and drove home. As we sat down to dinner, my dad, who had been my bishop during my teenage years, said: "Now, son, the first thing you want to do is get off to yourself and study the *General Handbook of Instructions* carefully; you need to know clearly what you can do and what you cannot do." It was good advice, and my study of that document is how I gained much of what I now know about Church government and procedures. "Wherefore, now let every man learn his duty, and to act in the office in which he is appointed, in all diligence" (D&C 107:99).

The second thing that we must learn to do if we are to truly acquit ourselves like priesthood men is not just to wrap our *minds* around our calling (to understand it, grasp its purposes, etc.) but, more important, to wrap *ourselves* around our calling. Elder Dallin H. Oaks has written of the significant labor, adjustment of orientation, and introspection through which he passed when he was called to serve as a member of the Quorum of the Twelve Apostles: "Contemplating the way I would spend the rest of my life, I asked myself what kind of apostle I would be. Would I be a lawyer who had been called to be an apostle, or would I be an apostle who used to be a lawyer? I concluded that the answer to this question depended upon whether I would try to shape my calling to my own personal qualifications and experience, or whether I would undertake the painful process of trying to shape myself to my calling.

"Would I try to perform my calling in the world's ways, or would I try to determine and follow the Lord's ways?

"I made up my mind that I would try to change myself to fit my calling, that I would try to measure up to the qualifications and spiritual stature of an apostle. That is a challenge for a lifetime.

"This principle applies to all of us. In every area of the

Church, there are wonderful men and women who are struggling to shape themselves to the dimensions of their callings, making the changes necessary to measure up to their assigned responsibilities in the kingdom of our Lord and Savior, Jesus Christ.

"In contrast, we have all seen examples of persons who have been unwilling to shape themselves to a new calling, but who have insisted on trying to make the calling conform to their own experience, preference, or comfort. We have seen teachers in church classes who have not taught the assigned subject, but have substituted the subject matter with which they are most familiar from their occupation or their recent reading. We have observed officers in various church organizations who have persisted in performing the duties of their callings according to the procedures of their own occupations. And we have seen speakers or others with church assignments who have used their positions as a way of serving a personal interest (such as gratifying their ego) rather than acting as servants of the Good Shepherd, who has called us to feed the flock of God" (*Lord's Way*, 7–8).

The work in which we are engaged is the Lord's work, and we will succeed only to the extent that we do things his way and according to his revealed principles. We either operate by divine direction or we struggle, falter, and fail. Many years ago I sensed that a young man under my jurisdiction was wrestling with his faith. I asked him to meet with me during the week, but he didn't show. We rescheduled two or three times before he finally made it to my office a few weeks later. His countenance was dark. He was agitated, clearly irritated that he should need to answer to anyone, especially me. He stated that he no longer believed in the Church and was guilty of a very serious transgression, which he refused to disclose. I thought it odd that he wanted me to know that he had sin in his life but didn't desire to confess it. We met again a week later. He was the same bitter, antagonistic personality. I had prayed a great deal about this young man but had not come to any particular conclusion as to how to invite him to confess and how to help him climb back on course. He began to speak very condescendingly to me, explaining that he had read the standard works many times, had a deep knowledge of the teachings of the Church, but now found it all very unconvincing.

It was at this point in the conversation that a strong impression came to me. I said: "So you're ready to quit the Church and leave it all behind?"

He replied: "That's right. I just don't find the doctrines of Mormonism intellectually stimulating any more."

I felt to challenge, even push him a bit, and said, "I'm not sure you're as bright as you claim. I for one find the doctrines of the Book of Mormon to be extremely stimulating, worthy of a lifetime of reading and rereading. But I suppose you have missed most of the profundity within the Book of Mormon."

He shot right back, "I've read the Book of Mormon a

number of times, and I don't remember much about it that excited my mind."

I responded, "Well, that's what I mean. You don't remember much that's exciting. And I claim that it's brimful of doctrine and precepts that can challenge the brightest theologians. I suppose you're not willing to try reading it again, are you?"

He didn't like being challenged. "Why would I want to read it again?" he demanded.

I asked, "Are you afraid that you just might discover truths and gain insights that would compel you to think twice about your decision to leave the Church?"

"I'm not afraid of anything," he insisted.

"Then here's my challenge to you," I said. "I want you to read the Book of Mormon through in three weeks and come back to me and report."

"What do you want me to report on?" he asked.

I answered, "Report on the kinds of things I am convinced you will discover."

Strangely, he agreed and took the challenge.

I prayed and fasted during those three weeks. I pleaded with the Lord to confound the young man in his pride, assault his arrogance, and open his eyes to see and know that what was in his hands was more precious than silver and gold.

To be completely honest, I was quite nervous when he came back into my office three weeks later, not knowing what to expect. But what I witnessed before me was exactly what I had prayed for. His demeanor was entirely changed. He was calm, settled, and fairly humble.

"I did it," he announced. "I read the whole book in three weeks."

"What did you find?" I asked.

An uncomfortably long pause was followed by these words: "I haven't felt this way in a long, long time. I felt close to God. I know you told me not to mark anything, just to read, but I couldn't help it. I marked a whole lot of passages that seemed to jump off the page. I'm ready to talk to you about my sins." And he did.

We took appropriate disciplinary measures, met with him regularly as he worked through a thorough repentance, and finally was able to see him as a new man, a changed man, one who had taken the challenge to try the virtue of the word of God (Alma 31:5). This young man's Heavenly Father knew just what he needed and, thanks be to God, the Spirit communicated that need to his poor servant, who happened to be listening at the time. God spoke, and a new individual came into existence.

This is the business of the priesthood, the business of transforming souls, of leading men and women to have faith in the Lord Jesus Christ.

This is but one small illustration of how Deity can inspire us to acquit ourselves as men. Priesthood men stand and deliver. They exercise righteous influence. Men who would enjoy such influence kneel to learn the will of heaven and then walk the earth to bring to pass the mysterious but marvelous ways of God.

POINTS TO PONDER

1. What is a real man? What are some of the tender characteristics of the Son of Man of Holiness, as recorded in 3 Nephi 17?

2. What kind of man does my wife need and deserve as a husband?

3. What kind of man do my children need and deserve as a father?

4. What are some differences between a worldly man and a man of Christ, a priesthood man?

PREPARING TO MEET GOD

IN MARCH OF 1983, I MET WITH administrators at Brigham Young University for a final hiring interview. I had known about this meeting for about a month, and so I did not get a great deal of sleep during those weeks. Our bed in the master bedroom of our Athens, Georgia, home was fairly comfortable, but my mind could not keep from racing throughout the day, wondering what would be said, what would be expected, how I would come across, what would be decided.

Shauna and I were excited that things had progressed to this point, but we were also aware that the interview might not go well and that the Millets would remain in Athens. And we were okay with that. Our hearts had changed, our desires and ambitions had been surrendered to God, and we were prepared to be wherever the Lord wanted us. That didn't, however, keep me from feeling the anxiety associated with such a meeting.

I sat outside the president's office for about five minutes

before the appointed hour—nervously twiddling my thumbs, crossing and uncrossing my legs, and glancing at my watch about every thirty seconds. I arose three or four times and tip-toed over to the water fountain for a drink. Then suddenly the door opened, and I was invited into a room with the president and four vice presidents.

In preparation for this interview, I had thought deeply and tried to imagine what I might be asked. I knew the inter-viewers would probably ask about my doctoral studies, about my areas of specialty at Florida State, and about what areas I would like to research and publish in.

But I was not unmindful of other matters: BYU is the Church's flagship academic institution; it is supported gener-ously by the Church through precious tithing funds—the faithful offerings of widows and little children; parents throughout the Church send their children to BYU to be in-spired as well as informed, to receive an education that is as faith promoting as it is stimulating to the mind; and that those appointed to teach in Religious Education are expected to be, at their very core, men and women of faith and convic-tion. I knew, therefore, that the administration would be anxious to determine the depth of my spirituality, to accu-rately measure what they would *feel* in my presence and not just what they would *hear*.

As I sat in the meeting, listening to counsel and respond-ing to questions (including one vice president's favorite in-terview question: "What are some of the books you have read during the last year?"), it occurred to me that my month's worth of preparation—my mental constructions of what this would be like, as well as my rehearsal of answers, had been helpful but in many ways insufficient. I realized that I was what I was; I was what I had become. I could not feign brilliance or pretend to be some impressive intellectual that I was not. I could not don the robes of academic achievement if in fact my years of reading and study and reflection had been inadequate. And if I had not prepared myself by living the gospel and attempting to be true to my covenants, they would certainly see through any façade of false spirituality I might attempt to present. It was a stunning realization but one that brought peace to my soul and settled my fears. Heavenly Father knew things the way they were, and surely he would reveal the same to those who had weighty decisions to make. I was content, knowing things were in his hands.

We are linked forever to the inexorable law of the harvest: "Be not deceived," Paul wrote. "God is not mocked: for whatsoever a man soweth, that shall he also reap. For he that soweth to his flesh shall of the flesh reap corruption; but he that soweth to the Spirit shall of the Spirit reap life everlasting" (Galatians 6:7–8).

Alma called this the law of restoration: "The meaning of the word restoration is to bring back again evil for evil, or carnal for carnal, or devilish for devilish—good for that which is good; righteous for that which is righteous; just for that which is just; merciful for that which is merciful. Therefore, my son [Corianton], see that you are merciful unto your brethren; deal justly, judge righteously, and do good continually; and if ye do all these things then shall ye receive your reward" (Alma 41:13–14).

This is sound, practical counsel to the people of the covenant, and especially to you and me, for we hold the priesthood of Almighty God. We have been called to stand in his place, to represent him, to do and say what he would do and say if he were personally present. We therefore cannot be casual in our relationship with Deity in this life and expect to enjoy sweet communion with him and his Beloved Son after death and throughout eternity. We cannot be undisciplined in our choice of movies, television, music, and the Internet and expect to enjoy the blessings of dedicated discipleship, either here or hereafter. And we cannot be harsh, unkind, or aloof in our relationships with our wives and children while in this life and expect to enjoy the consummate privileges of eternal lives (D&C 132:24), which is the joyous continuation of the family unit in the great beyond. The truth is, we are now in the process of becoming the person we will be, either one qualified for glory and honor and everlasting life, or one qualified for "the deaths" (D&C 132:25)—the dissolution of the family unit and the judgment to live "separately and singly, without exaltation, in [our] saved condition, to all eternity" (D&C 132:17). We must choose. Will we be men of power or not? Preparation precedes power.

President Joseph Fielding Smith taught that "*procrastination,*

as it may be applied to gospel principles, is the thief of eternal life—
which is life in the presence of the Father and the Son"
(Conference Report, April 1969, 121; emphasis added). Elder
Lance B. Wickman has also pointed out that "death is a cur-
tain through which each must pass, and . . . none of us knows
when that passage will occur. Of all the challenges we face,
perhaps the greatest is *a misguided sense that mortality goes on forever. . . .* And the person we are when we depart this life is the
person we will be when we enter the next. Thankfully, we do
have Today" (*Ensign,* May 2008, 104–5; emphasis in original).

Similarly, Elder Neal A. Maxwell warned those who feel
they just might change, but not now: "Do not look too
deeply into the eyes of the pleasure-seekers about you, for if
you do you will see a certain sadness in sensuality, and you
will hear artificiality in the laughter of licentiousness.

"Do not look too deeply, either, into the motives of those
who deny God, for you may notice their doubts of doubt.

"Do not risk thinking the unthinkable, lest you find
yourself drawn with a deep and powerful pull toward the reality that God does exist, that he loves *you,* and that finally
there is no escaping him or his love! . . .

"Do not think, either, about the doctrine that you are a child
of God, for if you do, it will be the beginning of belonging. . . .

"Do not over-pack the luggage you plan to take with you
when you leave this world, for we simply cannot get most
mortal things by celestial customs; only the eternal things are
portable. . . .

"Indeed, one of the most cruel games anyone can play with self is the 'not yet' game—hoping to sin just a bit more before ceasing; to enjoy the praise of the world a little longer before turning away from the applause; to win just once more in the wearying sweepstakes of materialism; to be chaste, but not yet; to be good neighbors, but not now. . . .

"The truth is that 'not yet' usually means 'never.' Trying to run away from the responsibility to decide about Christ is childish. . . .

"And, if you sense that one day every knee shall bow and every tongue shall confess that Jesus Christ is the Lord, why not do so now? For in the coming of that collective confession, it will mean much less to kneel down when it is no longer possible to stand up!" (*Ensign*, November 1974, 12–13).

It was Amulek who counseled: "This life is the time for men to prepare to meet God; yea, behold the day of this life is the day for men to perform their labors" (Alma 34:32). And how do we prepare here to meet our God there? While there are as many suggestions as there are people to make them, consider: First, we must begin praying for and practicing everyday holiness. Our Heavenly Father is called Man of Holiness, and Jesus Christ is therefore the Son of Man of Holiness or simply the Son of Man (Moses 6:57). Holiness just may be the virtue, the attribute, the divine quality that best characterizes exalted and glorified beings. They are holy and have called us to the same holiness (Leviticus 11:44; 1 Peter 1:16), at least to begin the process in this life. To be holy is to be separate from uncleanness, from defilement, from that which stains and taints the soul. And a special command is given from the heavens to those of us on earth who have been called to labor as holders of the priesthood: "Go ye out from Babylon. Be ye clean that bear the vessels of the Lord" (D&C 133:5; see also 38:42; Isaiah 52:11). Moroni wrote poignantly about the horrible discomfort, even torment of standing in the presence of a holy being when we are filled with guilt, when we have set at naught the counsels of God (Mormon 9:1–5).

Second, we need to learn to communicate with our Heavenly Father *now*. We must pray always—in the morning, at night, and all throughout the day, pleading with our God to prompt us, guide us, and take the carnal cataracts away from our eyes that we may see. Remember: It's awfully hard to strike up and maintain a conversation with a stranger! We ought to be on speaking and listening terms with our gracious Father before we leave this sphere of existence. We will eventually pick up where we left off and continue a conversation that will be sublimely satisfying and instructive.

Third, we need to be more than superficially acquainted with the holy scriptures. If we are not now serious students of holy writ, it's time to get started. Men of the priesthood simply need to become gospel scholars. We need to know the word of the Lord, and we need to know where to find it. Our counsel, sermons, and our lessons should always be laced with scripture and prophetic statements. The language and logic of scripture should permeate our thoughts and our speech. It is vital as the Church grows and spreads to all lands that we as Latter-day Saints know our religion, know how to articulate its truths clearly and systematically, and that we not only have a testimony of its truthfulness but also be competent witnesses in proclaiming it. Further, scripture is a dynamic means by which the Lord communicates eternal truth to us. Holy writ is the source of individual revelation. "When we want to speak to God, we pray," Elder Robert D. Hales observed. "And when we want Him to speak to us, we search the scriptures; for His words are spoken through His prophets. He will then teach us as we listen to the promptings of the Holy Spirit" (*Ensign,* November 2006, 26–27).

Fourth and finally, we need to exercise our priesthood more often, participate in its ordinances as frequently as we have the opportunity, including during frequent attendance at the temple. Participation in temple ordinances immerses us in things of the Spirit and enables us to view the world through anointed eyes. In the temple, we hear and speak of, think about and reflect on, eternal things. Moreover, for me, being in the House of the Lord provides a sweet spirit of contentment and puts me in touch with my most cherished and noble feelings. I have noticed, for instance, that my wife never seems more beautiful to me than in the celestial room.

Further, we need to volunteer to give priesthood blessings without our wives or children having to ask for them; spiritual sensitivity and an eagerness to act in the stead of our great Head will bring an increased level of light into our hearts and homes. Why? Because it is "in the ordinances [of the priesthood that] the power of godliness is . . . manifest unto men in the flesh" (D&C 84:20).

As Alma explained, now is the day of our salvation. We cannot afford to wait until the next life to conduct ourselves as saved beings, nor can we depend upon taking some kind of spiritual quantum leap that will project us into glory. Rather, if we are quickened in this life by a portion of the celestial glory, we will, in the resurrection, receive a fulness of the same (D&C 88:29). It was Enos, son of Jacob, who spoke so eloquently of his anticipated meeting with his Master: "And I soon go to the place of my rest, which is with my Redeemer; for I know that in him I shall rest. And I rejoice in the day when my mortal shall put on immortality, and shall stand before him; then shall I see his face with pleasure" (Enos 1:27). The Prophet Joseph said the same of priesthood holders who magnify their callings and seek to embody virtue: "Then shall [our] confidence wax strong in the presence of God" (D&C 121:45). Enos concluded that such faithful servants will one day hear the Lord say to them, "Come unto me, ye blessed, there is a place prepared for you in the mansions of my Father" (Enos 1:27). God grant that it may be so for each of us.

POINTS TO PONDER

1. When will it be "too late" for me to prepare?
2. What are matters about which I have procrastinated,

perhaps for years, matters that if attended to would propel me off the spiritual plateau I am on?

3. What would I do today if I were asked to meet with the president of the Church tomorrow?

4. Although no one will feel completely prepared for death or for the Second Coming, what level of preparation do I feel will be acceptable to God?

AVOIDING LIGHT-MINDEDNESS

I HAVE FOUND THAT ONE OF THE most difficult things to do is to establish a life that is balanced—to be faithful without being obnoxious, to have certitude without arrogance, to be tolerant without being spineless. I have found it especially difficult to be happy and joyous, to be sociable and to have a healthy sense of humor, without losing control of my emotions and becoming light-minded. Obviously the Holy One of Israel is offended when we speak lightly of sacred things, profane the holy in a spirit of jest, or become vulgar or crude in our speech or humor. Consider what may happen in social gatherings when the hour is late, the mood light, our bodies and minds weary, and thus our emotional and spiritual restraints weakened. Before long something is said that causes a ripple of laughter, followed by more comments and more and more raucous laughter. Within a short time our emotional and spiritual control is seriously threatened.

Something deep down inside of us whispers that this is

not good, that there is something inappropriate about loud laughter and light-mindedness. And that's exactly what the Lord said to the Latter-day Saints. After having instructed the early Saints in regard to honoring the Sabbath, he counseled: "And inasmuch as ye do these things with thanksgiving, *with cheerful hearts and countenances, not with much laughter, for this is sin,* but with a glad heart and a cheerful countenance—verily I say, that inasmuch as ye do this, the fulness of the earth is yours" (D&C 59:15–16; emphasis added).

In the revelation designated by the Prophet Joseph as the "Olive Leaf," the Master likewise instructs us to "cast away your idle thoughts and your excess of laughter far from you." He goes on to direct, "Therefore, cease from all your light speeches, from all laughter, from all your lustful desires, from all your pride and light-mindedness, and from all your wicked doings" (D&C 88:69, 121). I believe the warning against "light speeches" and "light-mindedness" is a statement of divine concern regarding vanity or treating lightly the things of God, which vanity brings condemnation (D&C 84:54–55).

Though no people in all the wide world have more to be grateful for than the Latter-day Saints, though no one should be happier and more elated to be alive than the Latter-day Saints, there are limits of propriety in the outward expression of our joy, for "that which cometh from above is sacred, and must be spoken with care, and by constraint of the Spirit; and in this there is no condemnation" (D&C 63:64).

My mission president shared with me and other elders an experience he had with Elder Harold B. Lee. The two of them were invited to a luncheon in the Waldorf Astoria Hotel in New York City to which a number of other religious and civic leaders were invited. He said that the room was filled, the meal was superb, and the conversation around the room was light and lively. As the group was finishing eating, they noticed a rather large man just down the lengthy table from them push his plate forward and let out a boistrous "belly laugh," as my president called it. People all over the room ceased their chatter and turned to stare at the man. Elder Lee then leaned over to my president and whispered: "That man has just revealed the emptiness of his soul."

Toward the end of my mission I attended an all-mission conference in the old Jewish synagogue where we met for church in Manhattan. Elder Harold B. Lee also attended. We had a lovely meal, followed by entertainment provided by various elders and sisters. At a certain point in the program, two elders began to tell a series of funny stories, one after another, and the volume of laughter in the room began to rise. The experience my mission president and Elder Lee had had at the luncheon was still on my mind, so I glanced periodically at Elder Lee to see how he was taking it all in. He smiled here and there, and then, when the laughter seemed to reach its crescendo, I saw him lean over and whisper something to the president. After the evening was over and everyone had made their way out of the building, I walked with the president for a ways. "Do you mind if I ask you what Elder Lee whispered to you?" I ventured.

"He asked a question," he replied.

"What was the question?" I dared to ask.

Elder Lee asked: "When will the Latter-day Saints learn to smile?"

I was sobered once more.

I am too young (believe it or not) to have had extensive contact with President Harold B. Lee, but several of those who knew him best have shared with me that he had a delightful sense of humor. I have listened to many talks on tape, delivered by Elder Lee at general conference or at Brigham Young University devotionals or to the Church Educational System, that demonstrate that he loved life and knew how to find and identify humor and humorous events all about him. And yet he knew what was appropriate and what was not.

At the closing session of his first general conference as president of the Church, President Lee lovingly but firmly counseled the Church regarding the excess of laughter in a general conference meeting: "I wonder sometimes if we forget that all we say in this sensitive building is going out over the air from a sacred assembly. It doesn't mean that we should be long-faced, should not show our joy, but we ought to couch our expressions of joy not with the audible expression that swells up to a great crescendo that might be mistaken by those who are listening on the outside. I think it would be well for us to remember that, with a sense of our responsibility to the most high God" (*Ensign,* January 1973, 133–34).

Those who know me well know that I have something of a sense of humor, an ability to laugh at myself more than anything but also a capacity to recognize when something is funny. For many years I have tried to tone down my laughter and guard my jests strictly because I have such tremendous admiration for President Lee and thus for his counsel. President Lee was a true seer, one who in many ways had a phenomenal effect on the Church long before he became its eleventh president.

Some who now preside over us as apostles and prophets were trained and taught and tutored by him, and so his influence upon the kingdom continues. His knowledge of the scriptures, his openness and receptivity to the spirit of prophecy and revelation, his vision of what needed to be done and how it could be carried out—these are but a few of the myriad of gifts that President Lee exercised during his mortal ministry, and I cannot but believe that his contribution on the other side of the veil is at least as profound as it was here. Thus when someone of his spiritual stature—one of the noble and great ones, to be sure—expresses a concern or issues a kindly warning, I am eager to follow that counsel. Over the years, however, my willingness to hearken in this matter has begun to be motivated more by an inner witness than sheer obedience.

I have become fascinated by a word used quite often in scripture but one I had not attended to in the past as I should. The word is *sober.* Note the following passages from both the Bible and from latter-day scripture:

"Be not conformed to this world: but be ye transformed by the renewing of your mind. . . . For I say, through the grace given unto me, to every man that is among you, not to think of himself more highly than he ought to think; but to *think soberly, according as God hath dealt to every man the measure of faith*" (Romans 12:2–3; emphasis added).

"But ye, brethren, are not in darkness, that that day [the Second Coming] should overtake you as a thief. Ye are all the children of light, and the children of the day: we are not of the night, nor of darkness. Therefore *let us not sleep, as do others; but let us watch and be sober*" (1 Thessalonians 5:4–6; emphasis added; compare D&C 61:38).

"For the grace of God which bringeth salvation to all men, hath appeared; teaching us that, *denying ungodliness and worldly lusts, we should live soberly, righteously, and godly,* in this present world (JST, Titus 2:11–12; emphasis added).

"Wherefore *gird up the loins of your mind, be sober,* and hope to the end for the grace that is to be brought unto you at the revelation of Jesus Christ" (1 Peter 1:13; emphasis added; compare D&C 73:6).

"Now, my beloved brethren, I, Jacob, according to the responsibility which I am under to God, *to magnify mine office with soberness,* and that I might rid my garments of your sins,

I come up into the temple this day that I might declare unto you the word of God" (Jacob 2:2; emphasis added).

"But ye will teach them [children] to *walk in the ways of truth and soberness;* ye will teach them to love one another, and to serve one another" (Mosiah 4:15; emphasis added).

"And now, my son [Helaman], see that ye take care of these sacred things, yea, see that ye look to God and live. Go unto this people and *declare the word, and be sober*" (Alma 37:47; emphasis added; compare 38:15; 42:31).

"And they were all young men, and they were exceedingly valiant for courage, and also for strength and activity; but behold, this was not all—*they were men who were true at all times in whatsoever thing they were entrusted. Yea, they were men of truth and soberness,* for they had been taught to keep the commandments of God and to walk uprightly before him" (Alma 53:20–21; emphasis added).

"Behold, I do not condemn you; go your ways and sin no more; *perform with soberness the work which I have commanded you*" (D&C 6:35; emphasis added).

"*Take upon you the name of Christ, and speak the truth in soberness*" (D&C 18:21; emphasis added).

"Treasure these things up in your hearts, and *let the solemnities of eternity rest upon your minds. Be sober.* Keep all my commandments" (D&C 43:34–35; emphasis added).

In Joseph Smith's day, the word *sober* referred not just to freedom from intoxication but also to temperance (self-control); not being heated with passion; cool, dispassionate reason; and being regular, calm, serious, solemn, and grave (Webster, *American Dictionary,* s.v. "sober"). Latter-day Saints are by nature a happy people, and, as the Prophet Joseph Smith observed, "Happiness is the object and design of our existence" (*Teachings,* 255). King Benjamin taught that those who keep the commandments of God are "blessed in all things, both temporal and spiritual; and if they hold out faithful to the end they are received into heaven, that thereby they may dwell with God In a state of never-ending happiness" (Mosiah 2:41). Life can be fun, it can be enjoyable, and some things simply tickle our funny bone. But we are also a people who know who we are, why we are here, and where we are going hereafter. We know that some things matter, worlds more than other things.

In that sense we are serious, devoutly serious, about putting our lives in order as priesthood holders, serious about denying ourselves of ungodliness and worldly lusts, extremely serious about cultivating the gift of the Holy Ghost so that we might enjoy power in our lives, power in the priesthood, righteous influence within and beyond the Church. We are and should be serious when it comes to being a loving and faithful husband, a good father, and a caring neighbor. We are sober when it comes to accepting and carrying out the call to serve as a home teacher, a priesthood representative to certain families who definitely need a friend and to be nourished by the good word of God (Moroni 6:4). Such matters dare not be treated casually or taken lightly. The Lord does not want us to be miserable while engaged in his work; on the contrary, he desires that we feel the deepest of joys and the sublime peace that flow from righteous and obedient service.

We must never forget, however, that life is in fact a mission, not a career; that when all of the kingdoms of this world have been leveled to the ground, when all the terrible wrongs have been righted and the tables turned on the mischievous, the conniving, and the scorner, the cities of Zion will stand forever, populated by men and women who are pure in heart (D&C 97:21) and have yielded themselves unto their Lord and Master (Helaman 3:35). We are about the business of the salvation of souls (our own included), and that is serious business. We are about the business of enjoying priesthood power in our homes, and that is very serious business. And, finally, as people of the covenant we are very much involved in trying to be the salt of the earth and the light of the world (D&C 101:39–40), a royal priesthood, anxiously engaged in transforming a people and preparing them for the supernal reign of the King of kings and Lord of lords. In short, our enjoyment of life must never cloud our vision of the eternal significance of life.

POINTS TO PONDER

1. Am I sensitive enough to recognize when my laughter is beyond the limits of propriety?

2. Am I open and teachable enough to ask others whom I

trust to assist me in assessing the propriety of my humor? Whom would I contact?

3. What is the difference between being giddy and being joyous?

4. When will I learn to smile without becoming boisterous in my laughter?

PROTECTION AGAINST PRIDE

AN INSPIRED LETTER WRITTEN BY THE Prophet Joseph Smith from Liberty Jail attests that many are called but few are chosen because men's hearts are too often "set so much upon the things of this world, and aspire to the honors of men" (D&C 121:35). In other words, they have not learned the lesson of the ages: that the rights of the priesthood are inextricably linked to the powers of heaven. In addition, we are told that whenever a man who has been ordained seeks to cover his sins or to gratify his pride or vain ambition, "the heavens withdraw themselves; the Spirit of the Lord is grieved; and when it is withdrawn, Amen to the priesthood or the authority of that man" (D&C 121:37).

We have spoken already of vain ambition. Now let us turn our attention to the granddaddy of all sins, the source of much if not all sin. "There is one vice of which no man in the world is free," C. S. Lewis remarked, "which every one in the world loathes when he sees it in someone else; and of which hardly any people . . . ever imagine that they are guilty them-selves. . . .

"The vice I'm talking of is Pride or Self-Conceit: and the virtue opposite to it, in Christian morals, is called Humility. . . . According to Christian teachers, the essential vice, the ut-most evil, is Pride. Unchastity, anger, greed, drunkenness, and all that, are mere fleabites in comparison: it was through Pride that the devil became the devil: Pride leads to every other vice: it is the complete anti-God state of mind" (*Mere Christianity*, 109–10).

Strong language, to be sure. But very real. Very much alive and well on planet Earth as well as within our own little uni-verses of activity. Lewis goes on to describe pride as follows: "Pride gets no pleasure out of having something, only out of having more of it than the next man. We say that people are proud of being rich, or clever, or good-looking, but they are not. They are proud of being richer, or cleverer, or better looking than others. . . . Once the element of competition has gone, pride has gone." Finally, "Pride always means enmity—it *is* enmity. And not only enmity between man and man, but enmity to God" (*Mere Christianity*, 110–11).

Many years ago I sat on the stand in a sacrament meet-ing. I had been asked to be the concluding speaker in an ad-joining ward. The young woman who spoke before I did was probably about sixteen years of age and quite impressive. Her topic was timely, her remarks were well thought through, her presentation was wonderfully organized, and her use of pertinent scriptures was outstanding. In fact, she used the scriptures so much that I found myself turning with her to different passages, even when she didn't provide the references for the congregation.

I was really enjoying myself during her message, finding rich application to my own personal life and also refreshing my mind with a number of scriptures I hadn't browsed in some time.

I looked up at a certain point, looked over the members of the congregation, and noticed that a surprisingly large number of them were *watching me*—watching me turn with the speaker to the various passages. I thought to myself, *What a fascinating process we have going on here.* She would make a point, turn to the Book of Mormon or Doctrine and Covenants or New Testament, and I would immediately turn with her, and then I would notice out of the corner of my eye the members of the ward smiling, pointing slightly at me, and enjoying the show. This went on for about five to seven minutes.

What an impressive example I am setting, I thought. I was demonstrating how wonderful it is to know the scriptures so well that I could turn to verses or chapters even when the speaker did not cite an exact reference. Then the unexpected happened.

Without warning, the young woman turned to a passage in the Old Testament, began reading it, and I realized I hadn't the foggiest idea where she was. And so I had a decision to make, an instantaneous decision. It was made. I turned to the Old Testament—it didn't sound like anything I could remember from the triple combination or the New Testament—flipped through a few pages, pointed to a verse in the middle of nowhere, smiled, and nodded my head knowingly. I was playing El Bluffo: I had no idea where to turn, but I couldn't let my audience down!

Now, almost thirty years later, I still feel completely foolish for my actions. I was demonstrating a prideful heart. I was seeking an audience, pretending to know more than I did, distracting others from the speaker's message, and polluting my own heart through duplicity. I was guilty of the sin about which the Savior warned in the Sermon on the Mount—the sin of pride as demonstrated by doing what we do for the wrong reasons, to invite the accolades of others. Truly, I had had my reward (Matthew 6:1–8, 16–18).

The natural man within each of us desires to be petted, patted, and pampered. The natural man seeks praise, seeks followers, seeks always to be right, asserts an inordinate independence, takes his cues from the world rather than from the Lord, and, of course, strives slavishly to be Number One. Because he is painfully competitive, he tries desperately to upstage anything and everything else, to be the center of attention and the focal point of everyone else's world. The natural man is not only an enemy to God (Mosiah 3:19), working at cross purposes to the Father's great plan of happiness, but also an enemy to himself, working against his own personal happiness, his own best good (Alma 41:10–11). The natural man's plight is pitiful and pathetic. His end is spiritual shrinkage, emptiness, and unhappiness.

Have you ever noticed how difficult it is to accept compliments from others? Through the years that I have been associated with teaching, many people have come forward following a sermon or a lesson to thank me, and often they have taken the time to compliment me on my presentation. For a long time I struggled with this awkward moment and actually found myself arguing with the complimenting person, insisting that what I did was unimpressive and plain. In response to "Brother Millet, I enjoyed your lesson very much" I might say, "Oh, it wasn't really very good. I didn't cover half of the material, and what I did cover was not very well presented." I suppose my response was some brand of false modesty or perhaps a prideful attempt to elicit even more praise.

My wife, Shauna, watched and listened to this typical reaction for several years and then suggested I might try something novel: simply say, "Thank you." That was a good solution, until I began to realize something—that if in fact we did have a great growing experience together, that if the Spirit of the Lord had touched hearts and motivated people to greater righteousness, I was not the one to thank. Consequently, I began, more and more often, to say something such as, "There *was* a great spirit here tonight, wasn't there?" or "The Lord was good to us today, wasn't he?" My words were a simple effort to deflect the honor and the glory to the Source, to acknowledge, as Jesus taught, that "there is none good but one, that is, God" (Matthew 19:17).

My experience, then, has taught me that those who have been called to labor cannot afford to become mired in pride. Unchecked, pride will gradually destroy us as individuals and certainly dilute the spiritual influence we might have among our brothers and sisters. What can we do as priesthood holders to avoid pride and self-conceit as the plagues that they are? What can we do to point our minds and focus our attention away from ourselves and instead look to God and live? Consider the following suggestions:

First, whenever a blessing or a fortunate incident occurs in our lives, be quick to thank God. Take the time, where possible, to drop to your knees and express immediate gratitude. "Thou shalt thank the Lord thy God in all things," the revelation enjoins. Further, "And in nothing doth man offend God, or against none is his wrath kindled, save those who confess not his hand in all things, and obey not his commandments" (D&C 59:7, 21). But let's be clear about something: the Lord does not *need* our thanks. He is not in some way deficient in his feelings of worth. He loves us, he desires that we serve and obey him, but he will remain God if we should deny and defy and fight him to the bitter end. It is *you and I* who need to thank him. It's good for our soul to look outside and beyond ourselves and never be guilty of conceit or self-congratulatory attitudes or behavior.

In that spirit, we can, secondly, take the wise counsel of President Henry B. Eyring to record regularly what the Lord has done for us that day or that week: "My point is to urge you to find ways," he said, "to recognize and remember God's kindness. It will build your testimonies. . . .

"The key to the remembering that brings and maintains testimony is receiving the Holy Ghost as a companion. It is the Holy Ghost who helps us see what God has done for us. It is the Holy Ghost who can help those we serve to see what God has done for them" (*Ensign,* November 2007, 67–68). Memory is a powerful teaching device. Reading and rereading how our loving Father and beneficent Savior guided, protected, prospered, forgave, prompted, or empowered us is the equivalent of having a vigorous spiritual workout; it bends our knees, stretches our souls, and expands our hope.

Third, we should never think of the priesthood as *our* authority; rather, it is God's almighty power, loaned to us for a time and a season, to see how we will receive it, magnify callings within it, and share its blessings with those about us. God is our Principal, and we are his agents (D&C 64:29), his stewards, his under shepherds. As we grow gradually into the pure love of Christ, we find ourselves seeking out those who need to be blessed. "A man filled with the love of God," the Prophet Joseph Smith explained, "is not content with blessing his family alone, but ranges through the whole world, anxious to bless the whole human race" (*Teachings,* 174). "There is a love from God," the modern seer also declared, "that should be exercised toward those of our faith, who walk uprightly, which is peculiar to itself, but it is without prejudice; *it also gives scope to the mind, which enables us to conduct ourselves with greater liberality towards all that are not of our faith, than what they exercise towards one another.* These principles approximate nearer to the mind of God, because [they are] like God, or Godlike" (*Teachings,* 147; emphasis added).

Finally, we should remember that true humility is not self-effacing, false modesty but rather being inspired to see things as they really are—who God is and who we are. The prayer of the righteous Elisha in behalf of his young ministerial companion is so appropriate for those who are called to labor: "Lord, I pray thee, open his eyes, that he may see" (2 Kings 6:17).

Indeed, "pride is the universal sin, the great vice," President Ezra Taft Benson testified. "Pride is the great stumbling block to Zion" (*Ensign,* May 1989, 7). Rather than being caught up with ourselves, my earnest prayer is that we will be caught up in the love and tender mercies of the Holy One of Israel. Rather than constantly taking our emotional temperature to ascertain whether our self-esteem is in place, my hope is that we will seek for and obtain Christ-esteem, that we will rejoice, as Benjamin counseled us, in the goodness, majesty, and might of our Divine Redeemer (Mosiah 2:19–21; 4:11–12). And rather than gloating in our goodness and constantly displaying our mortal medals, my longing is that we will hold up Him who is the Light of the World (3 Nephi 18:24), a light that shines in darkness and spreads its influence wherever it is allowed to be.

Those with power in the priesthood, those whose influence for good is being felt, have learned to rely, not upon the arm of flesh or the principalities and powers of this telestial world, but rather upon the Source; therefore they have a view of the Atonement and the great plan of happiness that makes them Christ-centered, faith-centered, and grace-centered. And one who perpetually proclaims the magnificence of the Messiah will seldom have to grapple with the pitiable plight of those who yield to pride.

POINTS TO PONDER

1. C. S. Lewis has referred to pride as the great sin. In what ways does pride underlie lesser imperfections and misdeeds in my life?

2. What are some ways I could recognize pride in my speech, my attitudes, and my actions?

3. Humility is the antidote to pride. How can I develop humility? What do the scriptures teach?

4. Why would it be that the closer I come to God the more humble I become and the less prone I am to pride?

PRAY WITHOUT CEASING

As HOLDERS OF THE PRIESTHOOD of our Lord, our prayer life—including how we pray, how often we pray, how earnestly we pray, and how trustingly we pray—is an unerring measure of our personal spirituality. No man enjoys the power of the Holy Spirit or the powers of the priesthood who does not speak to, call upon, thank, supplicate, and petition his Father in heaven on a regular and ongoing basis. Indeed, no person ascends the mountain of spirituality who does not lift his voice and his heart in prayer to the Almighty.

Why do we pray? First, we believe our Heavenly Father knows us, individually, and has infinite love and tender regard for each of us. He feels. He yearns. He hurts and experiences sorrow over our rebellion, struggles, and our wanderings. He delights in our successes. He also responds to petitions and pleadings. He is neither untouchable nor unapproachable. Thus our prayers allow us to express to God our needs, our challenges, our deepest feelings and desires, and to ask sincerely for his help.

The more prayerful a man or a woman becomes, the more dependent he or she is upon God and thus the more trusting and reliant upon spiritual powers beyond their own. Prayer therefore builds spiritual strength by pointing us beyond our limited resources to Him who has all power. In short, we pray to better understand who we are and who God is. We pray to better understand what we can do on our own and what we can do only with divine assistance.

Second, prayer allows us to communicate with Deity, to open ourselves to conversation with divinity. If indeed the quality of a person's life is largely a product of the kinds of associations he cultivates, then we may rest assured that a man or woman who spends much time in prayer will in time blossom in personality and rise above pettiness, littleness of soul, and mortal jealousies and fears. One cannot have regular contact with influences that are degrading without being affected adversely. On the other hand, persons who regularly call upon God, pour out their souls in prayer, and yearn for genuine communion with Deity—such persons cannot help but be elevated and transformed by that association. The very powers of God, coming to us through his Holy Spirit, make us into men and women of purpose, of purity, of power and influence. In short, we pray in order to receive an infusion of power, to draw strength from an omnipotent Being.

There are certain roadblocks or barriers to communion

with the Infinite, things that get in the way and prevent us from enjoying the kind of closeness with our Heavenly Father that we could have. We all could volunteer examples of such roadblocks. Let me suggest but a few.

Surely no roadblock is more prevalent than distraction and preoccupation. When it is time to pray, we must put aside the things of the world, even good things, in order to engage the greatest good. We do not rush into the divine presence, any more than we would rush into the office of the president of the Church or the president of the United States. It is often helpful, before we begin to pray, to slow down, stop what we're doing, sit quietly, listen to inspiring music, read several verses of scripture, and ponder and reflect on what we are about to do—literally approach the throne of God.

Another roadblock to an effective prayer life is duplicity or trying to lead two disparate lives. Thus we would suppose that a person who is worldly throughout the day would have great difficulty praying effectively at night. Elder Howard W. Hunter observed: "Henry Ward Beecher once said: 'It is not well for a man to pray cream and live skim milk.' That was a century ago. There is now before us a danger that many may pray skim milk and live *that* not at all" (*Ensign,* November 1977, 52). Just as our lives are only as good as our prayers, so our prayers are only as good as our lives. That is, the more faithful we become in keeping the Lord's commandments and putting first things first, the more we open the doors of communication with the heavens and the more comfortable we feel with holy things and holy beings.

One of our most common shortcomings is to say our prayers regularly but to do so without much thought, reflection, or devotion, except when we suppose that we really need God's help. Elder Hunter explained: "If prayer is only a spasmodic cry at the time of crisis, then it is utterly selfish, and we come to think of God as a repairman or a service agency to help us only in our emergencies. We should remember the Most High day and night—always—not only at times when all other assistance has failed and we desperately need help. If there is any element in human life on which we have a record of miraculous success and inestimable worth to the human soul, it is prayerful, reverential, devout communication with our Heavenly Father" (*Ensign,* November 1977, 52).

A practice that I have found particularly beneficial—especially when I find myself just reciting words instead of really communing with God—is to devote myself to a prayer in which I ask the Lord for absolutely nothing but instead only express sincere gratitude for my blessings. This kind of prayer pays remarkable dividends and settles the soul as few other efforts (Bednar, *Ensign,* November 2008, 42).

Coach Vince Lombardi wisely observed that fatigue makes cowards of us all. Fatigue also makes it extremely difficult to enjoy our prayers. Perhaps it is not always wise to make our prayers the last thing we do each day. It may be worthwhile to occasionally have prayer well before going to bed, while our minds and bodies are in a mode to do more than utter a few well-worn and familiar phrases. There have been several times over the years when one or two of the children have talked me into watching a late movie with them, perhaps on a Friday night. It seemed to me at the time as though I would inevitably either fall asleep on the floor or on the couch. More than once I have gone into my bedroom, closed the door, and had a meaningful prayer before going downstairs to watch the movie.

Two keys to meaningful prayer, even public prayer, are sincerity and simplicity. We have no one to impress, no one's judgment to fear. Our words are addressed to Him who knows all things, including the desires of our hearts (D&C 6:16). It is thus wise to speak the words that we really feel. In Shakespeare's play *Hamlet*, Claudius stopped praying because his heart was simply not in his prayers. He said: "My words fly up, my thoughts remain below; / Words without thoughts never to heaven go" (act 3, scene 3.) The Prophet Joseph Smith taught in regard to prayer: "Be plain and simple, and ask for what you want, just like you would go to a neighbor and say, 'I want to borrow your horse to go to the mill'" (in Andrus and Andrus, *They Knew the Prophet*, 100). As a part of his own prayer to God, Zenos exclaimed: "Yea, thou art merciful unto thy children when they cry unto thee, to be heard of thee and not of men, and thou wilt hear them" (Alma 33:8).

I hope as we are called upon to pray that we will slow

down, take our time, and pray from our hearts. I am often pained as people hurry through a prayer as though it were a formality or something that needed to be dispensed with as quickly as possible. This is particularly true for the closure of the prayer. Sometimes people are so eager to be done with the prayer that they race through the name of Jesus Christ as though they were sprinting toward a finish line. This cannot be pleasing to our Lord's Father, who is also our Father. We should end our prayers with the dignity and transcendent respect deserved by the One who suffered for our sins and ransomed us with his blood, even the Savior of all humankind. If you and I will pray sincerely, from our hearts, speaking our words soberly and distinctly—especially the concluding words, "in the name of Jesus Christ"—we will begin to feel a power and a sacred influence in our lives that attests that the Lord hears us and is pleased with us.

One of the things most needed in our prayer lives is regularity. Some people find it helpful to pray in the same place. One man I know set aside a special place in his home, a place that over the years came to be like unto a personal sacred grove. When he entered that room he naturally felt a hallowed presence because over the years he had experienced there some of the most profound insights and some of the sweetest feelings and impressions of his life. That room had become for him, almost a holy of holies within his own home.

Almost fifty years ago a man taught me something that

changed my life. He said simply: "When you get out of bed in the morning, never let your feet touch the floor first. Always let your knees touch first." I recommend that bit of practical wisdom to you, especially if you find it difficult to have a regular, meaningful morning prayer. I have been surprised at how many people who would never, ever consider going to bed without praying in the evening have not managed to develop a habit of saying morning prayers. Perhaps my practical side comes through here, but I have thought that there are very few harmful or hazardous things that could happen to me between the time I lay my head on the pillow at night and the time I get up the next morning. But there are many challenges and temptations and decisions I must face throughout the day, and I need all the help I can get. From my point of view, evening prayers are extremely important, but morning prayers are vital.

There are prayers, and then there are prayers. Sometimes our prayers are joyful expressions of gratitude. On other occasions we may need some heavy burden to be lifted. At other times, we long for the kind of spiritual contact and close association that demands our most strenuous and disciplined efforts. Jacob of old wrestled with an angel until the breaking of day and thus obtained a blessing from God (Genesis 32:24–32). Hungering and thirsting after righteousness, Enos wrestled with the Lord in prayer all day and into the night, until the holy voice declared that his sins were forgiven (Enos 1:1–8).

Even our Lord and Savior came to know something about prayer that he could not have known before his sojourn in mortality. In the Garden of Gethsemane the Savior began to feel the loss of his Father's sustaining Spirit. "And being in an agony," Luke records, "he prayed more earnestly" (Luke 22:44). In his reflection on this singular occasion, Elder Bruce R. McConkie observed: "Now here is a marvelous thing. Note it well. The Son of God 'prayed more earnestly'! He who did all things well, whose every word was right, whose every emphasis was proper; he to whom the Father gave his Spirit without measure; he who was the only perfect being ever to walk the dusty paths of planet earth—the Son of God 'prayed more earnestly,' teaching us, his brethren [and sisters], that all prayers, his included, are not alike, and that a greater need calls forth more earnest and faith-filled pleadings before the throne of him to whom the prayers of the saints are a sweet savor" (in *Prayer*, 8).

Indeed, some thorns in the flesh call forth prayers of great intensity (2 Corinthians 12:7–10)—supplications and pleadings that are certainly out of the ordinary. Such vexations of the soul are not typical, not part of our daily prayer life. Just as it would be a mistake to suppose that Jacob or Enos wrestled with God in prayer every day, we should not suppose our every prayer requires the maximum, soul wrenching exertion that may be needed on other occasions. Occasionally, however, we must pass through the fire in order to come through life purified and refined and thus prepared to dwell one day in everlasting burnings with God and Christ (Isaiah 33:14).

If we are willing to move beyond a casual relationship with God, willing to spend the time and exert the energy necessary to make of our prayer life something more than it is now, then great things await us. Over time and with experience, our prayers can become more than petitions, as important as it is to petition the Lord. Our prayers can become instructive, the means whereby God can reveal great and important things to us. The apostle Paul taught us that "the Spirit also helpeth our infirmities: for we know not what we should pray for as we ought: but the Spirit itself maketh intercession for us with [strivings] which cannot be [expressed]" (Romans 8:26; see Smith, *Teachings*, 278; compare 3 Nephi 19:24; D&C 46:30; 50:29–30; 63:65). That is to say, if we are quiet and attentive, the Spirit of the Lord can, on some occasions, lead us to pray for things that were not on our personal agenda, deep things, things that pertain more to our eternal needs than our temporal wants. In such settings we may find our words reaching beyond our thoughts, praying for people and circumstances and eventualities that will surprise us. President Marion G. Romney was fond of saying: "I can always tell when I have spoken by the power of the Holy Ghost, because I learn something from what I have said." And so it is with praying in Spirit.

"God sees things as they really are," Elder Neal A. Maxwell wrote, "and as they will become. We don't! In order to tap that precious perspective during our prayers, we must rely upon the promptings of the Holy Ghost. With access to that kind of knowledge, we would then pray for what we and others should have—*really* have. With the Spirit prompting us, we will not pray 'amiss.'

"With access to the Spirit, our circles of concern will expand. The mighty prayer of Enos began with understandable self-concern, moved outward to family, then to his enemies, and then outward to future generations" (in *Prayer*, 45).

We kneel before God to show our reverence toward him. Where possible, we speak our prayers aloud. But many times in the day we are not in a position to kneel or to give audible voice to our yearnings or our feelings. And so it is that we have the commission to "pray always," to keep a prayer in our hearts, to speak to the Almighty in our minds. We pray for his direction and his strength in our work, in our studies, in counseling with troubled friends or confused loved ones, and even in our recreational pursuits. Amulek delivered this invitation: "Yea, cry unto him for mercy; for he is mighty to save. Yea, humble yourselves, and continue in prayer unto him. Cry unto him when ye are in your fields, yea, over all your flocks. Cry unto him in your houses, yea, over all your household, both morning, mid-day, and evening. Yea, cry unto him against the power of your enemies. Yea, cry unto him against the devil, who is an enemy to all righteousness. Cry unto him over the crops of your fields, that ye may prosper in them. Cry over the flocks of your fields, that they may increase. But this is not all; ye must pour out your souls in your closets, and your secret places, and in your wilderness. Yea, and when you do not cry unto the Lord, let your hearts be full, drawn out in prayer unto him continually for your welfare, and also for the welfare of those who are around you" (Alma 34:18–27; see also 37:36–37).

As Elder Boyd K. Packer pointed out some years ago, the moral pollution index in our society is rising (*Ensign*, May 1992, 66). Evil is on the loose. Satan is abroad in the land (D&C 52:14). I do not consider myself any stronger than anyone else. I cannot resist the incessant pull of immorality nor escape the desensitization that follows naturally from larger doses of harshness, crudeness, and violence without the infusion of spiritual power that comes through communion with the Infinite. I would suggest that the same thing is true for you. No one of us is invulnerable to satanic influences. No one of us is strong enough to confront the enemy alone.

An incident recorded in the Book of Mormon has fascinated me for years. After Alma the Elder had been converted to Christ and to the gospel through the preaching of Abinadi, he began to teach the word with great power. Drawn to Alma's teachings, people began to gather and form themselves into a body of believers in the wilderness near the waters of Mormon. Alma went into the water, and Helam presented himself to be baptized. Before performing the sacred ordinance that places one on the strait and narrow path, however, Alma cried out in prayer to his Maker: "O Lord, *pour out thy Spirit upon thy servant, that he may do this work with holiness of heart*" (Mosiah 18:12; emphasis added). Then he pronounced a baptismal prayer and immersed Helam in the water.

What a model for each one of us who bears the holy priesthood! What a pattern and an example for those of us who are called upon to officiate in the ordinances of the priesthood! No one of us desires to do anything to damage another's faith or disturb their peace. Nor do we want simply to go through the motions when we bless a baby or anoint the sick or dedicate a grave or baptize or confirm. Presuming to deal with people's souls is serious business. We need the Spirit of God to attend us when we act in the priesthood. We need divine inspiration and power from heaven when we stand in the place of our Lord and Master in administering the ordinances of salvation to others. In this regard, Joseph Smith wrote: "Thy mind, O man! If thou wilt lead a soul unto salvation, must stretch as high as the utmost heavens, and search into and contemplate the darkest abyss, and the broad expanse of eternity—thou must commune with God. How much more dignified and noble are the thoughts of God, than the vain imaginations of the human heart! None but fools will trifle with the souls of men" (*Teachings,* 137).

Each of us can refine and purify our lives through a greater attention to the regularity, intensity, and overall quality of our prayers. We who have been called to labor must learn to pray without ceasing, to commune with the Infinite when we are thrilled as well as when we are devastated, to give utterance to our souls' deepest longings when we have been prospered as well as when we have been humbled to the dust. We who are agents must communicate consistently with our divine Principal in order to ensure that what we say and what we do is just exactly what he would have said and done (D&C 64:29). We are on his errand and need to stand with confidence and nobility in his mighty cause, knowing, no matter the enormity of the ranks of the enemy, God is with us.

POINTS TO PONDER

1. How would I assess my prayer life? What might the Lord want me to do to make my prayers more meaningful?

2. How often do I pause after my prayer, clear my mind and heart, and listen for promptings or guidance?

3. What is something I recently prayed for? What have I done, as an act of faith, to help that prayer to be answered?

4. What lessons do I learn from the fact that the resurrected, glorified, immortalized Savior prayed to the Father often during his ministry among the Nephites, as recorded in 3 Nephi?

9

ABIDING IN TRUTH

MORE THAN TWENTY YEARS AGO one of my Brigham Young University students (let's call him Edward) knocked on my door and asked to speak with me. He was a handsome, well-built, and extremely bright young man who was only a semester removed from graduation. We chatted for several minutes about his family background, his overall BYU experience, and his plans for graduate school and the future. It was at this point that he shocked me with this announcement:

"Brother Millet, I don't know if I can go ahead and graduate from BYU."

"What do you mean?" I asked. "Why can't you graduate?"

He replied, "Because I don't feel good about being a BYU graduate with some of the feelings I have right now."

I asked him to elaborate, and he explained that he wasn't sure whether the Church was actually the Lord's Church, whether the Book of Mormon was in fact the word of God, and whether his full-time mission had perhaps been nothing more than a sham. "I love this school and feel deeply grateful for my teachers and what I have learned, and I just don't think it would be honest to accept a diploma and have these doubts about the truthfulness of Mormonism."

I had a scheduled appointment within minutes, and so we agreed to meet in a couple of days to consider his concerns in more detail.

It didn't take long with him before it was apparent that Ed had been perusing anti-Mormon propaganda and had become ensnared in a spirit of cynicism and doubt. He posed one anti-Mormon issue after another, and I quietly responded. After well over an hour of this, I decided it was time to do some probing and get to the heart of the matter. I found within minutes that the real problem was the Book of Mormon. Edward admitted that he had never really taken the time to pray for a spiritual witness of the truthfulness of the Book of Mormon. Why should he, he had concluded, when, as some members of the Church had informed him, there are so many external evidences of its truthfulness? His recent exposure to material critical of the origins and historicity of the Book of Mormon had shaken his faith, a faith that he now learned was built on a shallow foundation.

I assured him that there were indeed many internal and external evidences for the Book of Mormon but that the only way, as the apostle Paul had taught, that a person could know of the things of God was by the power of the Spirit of God (1 Corinthians 2:11–14).

Edward and I began the slow and painful but satisfying experience of making a proper spiritual investigation of that sacred volume and eventually were able to paste him back together again.

This example highlights the need to be properly grounded in our faith, to have a witness and a conviction based on revelation. We can only abide in the truth when we know and have internalized the truth.

It reminded me of another occasion a few years earlier when I had attended a seminar in which a member of the Church made a presentation in which he sought to "prove" the truthfulness of Mormonism through the use of the Dead Sea Scrolls (Hebrew) and the Nag Hammadi codices (Coptic). I will never forget his opening statement: "Did you know," he asked, "that there are thousands of identifiable documents from antiquity that prove beyond any doubt that The Church of Jesus Christ of Latter-day Saints is true?"

I didn't know that, and I was in that business. I wondered where he would go during the remainder of his presentation.

I am certain that he meant well, that he fully intended to strengthen the witness of the Saints and their invited friends of other faiths. But what followed for several hours was a recitation of texts torn from their context, a parade of supposed similarities with LDS teachings, and much flattery—literally false expectations in terms of trusting in unsolid evidence—that sent many Saints scurrying away with a warped sense of which sources we could rely upon and which ones we could not. They were not properly grounded because they had only been fed half truths.

Elder Neal A. Maxwell once expressed his view that "all the scriptures, including the Book of Mormon, will remain in the realm of faith. Science will not be able to prove or disprove holy writ. However, enough plausible evidence will come forth to prevent scoffers from having a field day, but not enough to remove the requirement of faith. Believers must be patient during such unfolding" (*Plain and Precious*, 4).

Those who have been called to labor, those who have been ordained to act in His Holy Name, are expected to represent our Lord and Master. We cannot do so unless we know the truth and abide in that truth. To *abide* is to rest, to tarry, to continue permanently, and to remain (*Webster's Dictionary*, s.v. "abide"). This is what Jesus had in mind when he taught that those who continue in his word are truly disciples; they would know the truth, and the truth would set them free (John 8:31–32). God needs our hearts, our wills, our desires, our ambitions, our tenacity, our might, and our strength. He also needs our *minds,* and he needs us to use those minds most productively in spreading the word of salvation and reasoning lovingly and with civility with those who see things differently. We cannot teach what we do not know, any more than we can return to where we have never been. God's kingdom requires those who are steadfast and immovable (Mosiah 5:15), those who stay with the task of discipleship until they breathe their last breath, those who run the race of faith nobly and boldly, those who finish (Luke 9:57–62; 14:26–33), those whose loyalty to the Redeemer is grounded in a solid knowledge of his gospel and its principles and precepts.

Let's get right to the point: we as holders of the priesthood need to know the gospel and how to articulate the doctrines of the kingdom better than we do. Obviously it is vital that we live our lives in such a manner that our Christlike examples bespeak our true Christianity and our devotion to our Lord and Savior. President David O. McKay reminded us that every member of the Church should be a missionary, but the cause of the Restoration would move forward by leaps and bounds if every member were a true member! Our example is crucial. How we live what we profess will speak loudly in the ears of both critics and interested and genuine seekers of truth.

At the same time, we must, simply must, not only know the gospel is true but, foundationally, *we must know the gospel.* Doing so will not only empower us to effectively teach what we believe to those both within and without the Church, but it will also open us to the crucial guidance from our Principal that comes by the power of the Holy Ghost.

Elder Bruce R. McConkie pointed out to Regional Representatives and other Church leaders in April 1981 that "our tendency—it is an almost universal practice among most Church members—is to get so involved with the operation of the institutional Church that we never gain faith like the ancients, simply because we do not involve ourselves in the basic gospel matters that were the center of their lives.

"We are so wound up in programs and statistics and trends, in properties, lands, and mammon, and in achieving goals that will highlight the excellence of our work, that we 'have omitted the weightier matters of the law.' And as Jesus would have said: 'These [weightier things] ought ye to have done, and not to leave the other undone' (Matthew 23:23)....

"*However talented men may be in administrative matters; however eloquent they may be in expressing their views; however learned they may be in worldly things—they will be denied the sweet whisperings of the Spirit that might have been theirs unless they pay the price of studying, pondering, and praying about the scriptures*" (*Doctrines of the Restoration*, 236–38). Once again, one of the grand keys to the receipt of individual revelation is the careful and prayerful study of institutional revelation, namely, the holy scriptures.

Many years ago, while working as a full-time seminary teacher in Salt Lake City, one of my colleagues (let's call him Brad) and his wife were having great difficulty in having children. She had had several miscarriages, and this wonderful man and woman—who wanted more than anything to welcome little ones into their home—had known many years of grief and spiritual frustration. When she became pregnant again, they were very excited, as were we all. But complications arose once more, and the little boy was born some three months prematurely. His lungs were not fully developed, and the medical personnel in intensive care worked around the clock to keep him alive. We had all poured out our hearts in prayer and pleaded that divine powers might intervene and allow this child to live and grow and be raised by our friends.

One Friday evening, Shauna and I were just walking out the front door to go to dinner when the phone rang. I suggested that Shauna go ahead and get in the car and I would answer the phone. On the other end of the line was the humble and tender voice of my friend Brad.

"Bob," he said, "I wonder if I could ask a special favor of you?"

I said, "Certainly. How can I help?"

"As you know, our little guy is struggling to stay alive. We have given him more than one blessing, but I fear that I am so close to the situation that I just can't be spiritually objective, completely open to the mind of the Lord. Would you be willing to come up to the hospital in the next few minutes and give our baby a blessing?" He added, "We have confidence in your faith, and it would mean the world to us."

"Of course," I replied. "I'll be there shortly."

I went to the door, motioned to Shauna that I would be there soon, and retired to our bedroom, where I knelt in prayer. I felt the heavy burden of Brad's confidence and the solemnity of the moment, and so I knew I would need desperately to be guided in my words. I poured out my heart once again in behalf of my dear friends, begged for forgiveness of my sins and thus for an infusion of the power of God, in short, for power in the priesthood. Immediately I was wrapped in a blanket of peace and calm and assurance that the will of the Lord would be brought to pass and that I should not worry but proceed in confidence. I felt certain that the Lord would work a healing miracle through me. We drove to the hospital, took the elevator to the appropriate floor, and were taken by a nurse into the intensive care unit where baby, Mom, and Dad were located.

I dressed in the necessary hospital garb and spoke briefly to my friends. Then we made our way to the little fellow's bed. He was so tiny, so fragile, so near to the angels. Brad anointed the baby with oil, and then it was my turn. I called the child by name, stated my authority with enthusiasm and even volume, and said, calling him by name, "We lay our hands upon your head to seal the anointing you have received from a servant of the Lord, and say unto you . . ."

Nothing came. My mind went completely blank. No thoughts. No words. No idea as to what to do or say. The seconds ticked away, and I felt the uneasiness of my friend as he shuffled his feet a bit. I pleaded silently with the Lord: *Open my mind. Please, O God, teach me what to say. Tell me what to do. I am ignorant. I am weak and incapable.*

It seemed that an hour passed, though I suppose it was only thirty or forty seconds, and then suddenly my tongue was loosed, and I spoke: "We say unto you that if you are not appointed unto death, you shall be healed." I closed the blessing, for that was all that came to me. It was so odd, so unusual, so very awkward.

As we walked into the next room, Brad asked with much emotion in his voice, "He's going to die, isn't he?" I hesitated but then said, "Yes, I feel he is going to die. Soon." Which he did, only hours later. My heart ached with my friends' hearts. I grieved over their grief. As we sat down in the car, it occurred to me that I was clothed in feelings—pain, to be sure, but also a quiet form of gratitude. The reason for the pain is obvious. As to the gratitude, I was thankful that I had chosen in the months and years before that hour to search the scriptures, to immerse myself in the revelations of God. Why? Because what came into my mind at the time of the blessing—indeed, the only thing that entered—was a portion of a scriptural passage from the Doctrine and Covenants (42:48). As promised by our Redeemer, the Spirit had taught me through the medium of memory (John 14:26), had brought to my remembrance words delivered through the Prophet Joseph Smith.

Jesus the Christ is the Vine; we are the branches. We can do nothing, save we abide in him and rely wholly upon his tender mercies and enabling powers (John 15:1–5; 2 Nephi 31:19). We abide in truth by looking to Him who is the Truth (John 14:6). We abide in truth by searching the words of the prophets as found in holy writ. We abide in truth by listening to and studying and cross-referencing the words of modern apostles and prophets into our standard works and then teaching them. We abide in truth by *doing* truth, that is, by living truthfully (John 3:21; 1 John 1:6). We abide in truth through learning the gospel, preaching the gospel, and allowing the tenets of our faith to govern our attitudes and behavior. We abide in truth by fasting and praying and reading and memorizing the divine word, thereby becoming men of a sound understanding (Alma 17:1–3), men of incomparable influence. We abide in truth by being loyal to the royal within us.

POINTS TO PONDER

1. Do I structure my time so that every day contains a period of devotion, including a serious study of the scriptures?

2. If I were called upon by the leaders of the Church to teach the restored gospel to an important religious leader of another faith, how effective would my presentation be? What could I do to make it more effective?

3. Am I discovering in my gospel study that simple truths have become more profound to me? What are some of these truths?

4. How much time do I devote to the study of the general conference addresses in the *Ensign*? Have I begun to cross-reference some of these addresses into my scriptures?

TAUGHT BY THE COMFORTER

WHILE SERVING AS AN ELDERS quorum president in Idaho Falls during the early 1970s, I received a phone call at about 11:30 one night. Obviously calls at such a time cause you to jump out of bed and your imagination to run from north to south and east to west concerning what death in the family or other trauma must have occurred. I was relieved when I recognized the voice on the other end of the line as my quorum secretary. "Bob," he said, "sorry about the late hour, but my wife and I have been wrestling with a decision for the last few days, and we need to get some closure. We cannot go to bed until the decision is made—tonight."

"What can I do to help?" I asked.

"Well," Jim said hesitantly, "I would like to come over to your place and have you give me a blessing." I indicated that I would be very happy to do so but wondered what the issue was. "For some reason," he continued, "we think we should move to California."

"Well, this is an easy one," I shot right back. "We don't need to give you a blessing. I can tell you straight out that you are needed here, now, in this area. Does that do?"

Jim said, "I appreciate that, and we're ready to settle in right here, forever, if that's what the Lord wants. But would you give me a blessing confirming that?"

"Of course," I said. "Come on over."

I quickly dressed properly and prepared for the quiet knock on the door. Jim and I chatted together for quite a while. I assured him how very valuable he and Linda were to our ward but agreed to give him a blessing to settle things. I placed my hands on his head, called him by name, stated my authority, and within one minute instructed him, with a great feeling of urgency, to move to California and to do so just as quickly as he could. When "Amen" was said, Jim sat in his chair very still while I stood behind him with my hands on his shoulders for about a minute, and then we looked each other in the eyes. He grinned, I coughed, and Jim left the apartment as quickly as he had arrived. Within a few days his little family had packed up, moved on, and begun a new life in California.

Not long after arriving there, Jim entered into specialized training for a completely new field of employment and thereafter had a prosperous business. I look back at that evening, ponder on what took place, and marvel at how the Lord moves in mysterious ways his wonders to perform. Jim's was a simple request that had arisen because of a strong prompting. My rational refutation had quickly dismissed such crazy thinking, but my efforts to dissuade him were overturned because the One who presides over this Church and directs the affairs of those who trust him had spoken. Within a matter of moments an entire family's future was changed dramatically, but changed so as to be in harmony with divine purposes.

Because of the persecution and abuses the Saints had endured in Missouri, Joseph Smith the Prophet sought an audience with the president of the United States, Martin Van Buren. Among other things, Van Buren asked how Mormonism differed from other religious groups. The Prophet replied: "We [differ] in mode of baptism, and the gift of the Holy Ghost by the laying on of hands." All other considerations, Joseph continued, "[are] contained in the gift of the Holy Ghost" (*History of the Church*, 4:42). The distinctive characteristic of the Lord's people in all generations of time is the companionship of the Spirit and the manifestation of the gifts of that Spirit. Where that gift and those fruits are found, there truth and the authority that leads to salvation are found; where that gift and its attendant fruits are not found, there the church and kingdom of God are yet to be set up and established by the opening of the heavens.

The gift of the Holy Ghost is an evidence that the Higher Priesthood is on earth and that the powers to administer the gospel and unlock the mysteries of the kingdom are held by legal administrators called from on high. The Prophet himself taught that "no man can receive the Holy Ghost without receiving revelations. The Holy Ghost is a revelator" (*Teachings*, 328). A society of believers wherein the Holy Spirit has been bestowed is a society wherein the regular manifestations of prophecy and revelation abound. Such a people will profess not only the right but also the responsibility—and, of course, an attitude of openness and eagerness—to add to the canon of scripture and teach the importance of personal revelation, especially among those called to labor. The Holy Spirit is as the breath of life to The Church of Jesus Christ. While the canonized scriptures that have been bound together and accepted by the people as the word and will of the Lord is the penultimate source of truth, the final source, the ultimate authority, is Jesus Christ himself, working through the third member of the Godhead. "The risen Jesus, at the end of Matthew's Gospel, does not say, 'All authority in heaven and on earth is given to the books you are all going to write,' but [rather] 'All authority in heaven and on earth is given to me'" (Wright, *Last Word*, xi).

Growing in priesthood power is inextricably linked to cultivating the gifts and Gift of the Holy Ghost, the Comforter. If I am unworthy of the influence and direction of the Spirit, I am unworthy of the power to officiate in God's sacred authority. My influence is seriously limited. On the other hand, if I am earnestly striving to follow the course charted toward eternal life, striving to deny myself of all ungodliness, and seeking to be worthy of the companionship of the Holy Ghost, I will be empowered and inspired on what to do and say as a holder of the priesthood. Notice the language of a modern revelation: "And now I speak unto you, the Twelve—Behold, my grace is sufficient for you; you must walk uprightly before me and sin not. And, behold, you are they who are ordained of me to ordain priests and teachers; to declare my gospel, according to the power of the Holy Ghost which is in you, and according to the calling and gifts of God unto men" (D&C 18:31–32). Also: "Every elder, priest, teacher, or deacon is to be ordained according to the gifts and callings of God unto him; and he is to be ordained by the power of the Holy Ghost, which is in the one who ordains him" (D&C 20:60; compare Moroni 3:4). Or, as Joseph Smith explained, the Holy Ghost is "God's messenger to administer in all those priesthoods" (*Teachings,* 323.)

Matthew records that "it came to pass that Jesus grew up with his brethren, and waxed strong, and waited upon the Lord for the time of his ministry to come. And he served under his father [presumably, Joseph the carpenter], and he spake not as other men, *neither could he be taught, for he needed not that any man should teach him.* And after many years, the hour of his ministry drew nigh" (JST Matthew 3:24–26; emphasis added).

I'm fairly certain that this passage does not suggest that Jesus was untouchable or unteachable or that he was a stubborn or smart-aleck kid. Indeed, he no doubt was taught the Torah by his parents and by other knowledgeable persons in the community and thereby "increased in wisdom and stature, and in favour with God and man" (Luke 2:52). There were some things, however, he could only learn from his Heavenly Father or from the angels who ministered to him. So it is with us who bear the Holy Priesthood. John taught that "the anointing [the endowment of the Spirit] which ye have received of him abideth in you, and *ye need not that any man teach you:* but as *the same anointing teacheth you of all things, and is truth,* and is no lie, and even as it hath taught you, ye shall abide in him" (1 John 2:27; emphasis added).

We know that the Spirit will not dwell with those who are unclean and thus unworthy of its companionship (1 Corinthians 3:16–17; 6:19; compare 1 Nephi 10:21; 15:34; Alma 7:21; 3 Nephi 27:19). In addition, we cannot always tell when we will be filled with the Spirit and when we will not. Worthiness is only one variable. We may end the day on fire with the power of the Spirit, rejoicing in our blessings, grateful for the closeness we have felt to the Lord. When we arise a few short hours later, it would not be uncommon to feel as though we had lost something, to feel that the distance between us and Deity had increased dramatically.

We ask ourselves searchingly: "What happened? Did we sin during the night? Did we do something to change what we were feeling but a short time ago?" President Joseph F. Smith taught that "every elder of the Church who has received the Holy Ghost by the laying on of hands, by one having authority, has power to confer that gift upon another; *it does not follow that a man who has received the presentation or gift of the Holy Ghost shall always receive the recognition and witness and presence of the Holy Ghost himself, or he may receive all these, and yet the Holy Ghost not tarry with him, but visit him from time to time"* (*Gospel Doctrine*, 61; emphasis added). President Smith also observed that "the Holy Ghost may be conferred upon men, and he may dwell with them for a while, or he may continue to dwell with them in accordance with their worthiness, and *he may depart from them at his will"* (*Gospel Doctrine*, 466; emphasis added).

Because we cannot always *recognize* the workings of the Spirit in our lives is no guarantee that the Spirit is not with us. In looking back over the last thirty years of my life, it seems as though I have had a variety of experiences with the Spirit and with receiving answers to prayer. Many prayers have been answered so directly, so clearly, so unambiguously that there could be no doubt as to the course I should follow. On the other hand, I honestly admit that there have been many other times when I have gone before the Lord in deep sincerity, hungering and thirsting for insight and direction, when, so far as I could tell, I was not guilty of serious sin. I have pondered and prayed and pleaded and wrestled and waited upon the Lord on some of these occasions and yet a clear answer was not forthcoming.

President Brigham Young declared: "If I do not know the will of my Father, and what He requires of me in a certain transaction, *if I ask Him to give me wisdom* concerning any requirement in life, or in regard to my own course, or that of my friends, my family, my children, or those that I preside over, *and get no answer from Him, and then do the very best that my judgment will teach me, He is bound to own and honor that transaction,* and He will do so to all intents and purposes" (*Journal of Discourses,* 3:205; emphasis added).

I believe there is more to President Young's counsel than meets the eye. It is certainly true that we should pray with all our hearts for direction and then make the wisest decisions we can. It is my conviction, however, that even on those occasions when we feel so very alone—when we wonder if God is listening—if we are striving to be found worthy, the Lord is in fact directing our paths, for he has so promised us. No doubt there are certain seasons of our lives where we are called upon to proceed without the clear recognition of the Spirit. This does not mean that we are all alone. I believe that one day, when we are allowed to review the scenes of mortality from a grander perspective, we will be astounded at how closely the Lord directed our paths, orchestrated the events of life, and in general led us by that kindly light we know as the Holy Ghost.

Perhaps it is the case that over the years the Spirit of the Lord works in a quiet but consistent manner to educate our consciences, enhance our perspectives, and polish our individual wisdom and judgment. After all, the Prophet Joseph explained that one of the principal assignments of the Holy Ghost is to convey pure intelligence through expanding the mind, enlightening the understanding, and storing the intellect with knowledge (*Teachings*, 149). It may be that one day we will look back on what we perceived at the time to be seasons wherein we were required to make decisions on our own, only to discover that the Lord had been, through the honing and refining processes in our souls, leading us along in paths of his choosing. That is, maybe we will learn that our own wisdom and judgment were not really our own.

Finally, it is worth noting that one may well have an experience with the Spirit, a genuine and true experience, and yet not know exactly what had taken place (see 3 Nephi 9:18–20). Over the years it has been my privilege to work with many Latter-day Saints who were struggling to repent of their sins and become clean before God. It has been one of the joys of Church service to witness the light increasing in the countenance, the heart being softened, and the consciousness of right and wrong returning. Never, however, in all my years have I had a member of the Church say to me: "I have been justified of the Spirit" or "I have entered the rest of God" or "I am redeemed of the Lord" or "I am born of the Spirit." Those who have had their sins remitted and have renewed their covenant with Christ could, in fact, use any of those doctrinal phrases to describe their state or standing, and I would understand what they meant. Generally they say things such as: "I feel good all over" or "I feel clean and pure" or "I am at peace." Far more significant than a theological explanation is the value of a religious experience; whether we can give a ten-minute discourse on spiritual rebirth matters but little when compared to the change of heart that such a rebirth brings.

When my friend Joseph McConkie was called with his wife, Brenda, to preside over a mission in Scotland, they felt the need to somehow reduce or distil the "white handbook"—the book of mission rules—into a single principle. This was not because each of the regulations is not important but rather so that his missionaries might live their lives by principle rather than by an extended list of rules. This is what they adopted as a kind of mission motto: "I will never do anything that would cost me the influence of the Spirit of the Lord." What a consummate opportunity it is to have a precious association with a member of the Godhead. Other than salvation, which is the greatest of all the gifts of God in eternity and which comes through the infinite atonement (D&C 6:13; 14:7), the gift of the Holy Ghost is in fact the greatest of all the gifts of God in this life (Woodruff, *Discourses*, 5).

We honor our priesthood whenever we honor God and invite his Spirit into our daily walk and talk. Because the Comforter knows all things (D&C 42:17; Moses 6:61), we come to know things that God knows, line upon line and precept upon precept. God be praised for the gift of the Holy Ghost! If we enjoy its influence, we will be sanctified from the taints and stains of mortality. If we court its inspiration, it will lead us back home.

POINTS TO PONDER

1. What things have I come to understand with time and through divine inspiration that I could not have understood on my own?

2. How often do I pray regularly and intensely for the direction, perspective, cleansing power, and strength of the Spirit? If not, when will I begin?

3. What is the relationship between the power of the Holy Ghost and the power of the priesthood?

4. What additions and subtractions need to take place in my life in order to invite and cultivate the powers of the Spirit more consistently?

THE GIFT OF FAITH

NOT LONG AFTER I WAS ORDAINED an elder, my father was summoned to give a priesthood blessing. He grabbed me and said: "Come on, son. Let's take care of it." As we opened our car doors, Dad said: "Now, I want you to exercise all the faith you have." I nodded, but I was not completely certain what it meant to exercise faith. It just so happened that the young woman, who was about fourteen years of age and seriously ill, was my best friend's sister. I anointed, Dad sealed the anointing and gave a magnificent and inspired blessing; he promised her she would be made well very shortly. She was indeed. As we left their home and walked to the car, I felt weak, light-headed, and wobbly. And as we drove off, I said, "Dad, I don't feel very well. I have no strength." He smiled and told me a Bible story:

"And a woman having an issue of blood [hemorrhage] twelve years, which had spent all her living upon physicians, neither could be healed of any, came behind him, and touched the border of his garment: and immediately her issue of blood stanched [ceased]. And Jesus said, Who touched me? When all denied, Peter and they that were with him said, Master, the multitude throng thee and press thee, and sayest thou, Who touched me? And Jesus said, Somebody hath touched me: for I perceive that virtue is gone out of me. And when the woman saw that she was not hid, she came trembling, and falling down before him, she declared unto him before all the people for what cause she had touched him, and how she was healed immediately. And he said unto her, Daughter, be of good comfort [courage, cheer]: thy faith hath made thee whole; go in peace" (Luke 8:43–48).

Dad pointed out that Joseph Smith the Prophet had explained that the virtue that had "gone out of" Jesus was the spirit of life and that sometimes when men perform ordinances, such as blessing children or healing the sick, so much of the spirit of life is imparted in the blessing that the officiators become weak (*Teachings,* 280–81). In fact, there have been many occasions when the persons I was counseling, disciplining, or blessing seemed almost to have drawn strength from me—their faith was so sincere, so pure, so powerful that I felt as though a part of me had been transferred elsewhere. This is no doubt associated in some way with the Prophet's instructions to the School of the Elders that faith is "a principle of power." Faith is "the principle by which Jehovah works, and through which he exercises power over all temporal as well as eternal things" (*Lectures on Faith,* 1:15–16).

A modern-day application of the above New Testament scene was described movingly by Elder Joseph B. Wirthlin: "Over 1,200 people, Saints and investigators, came from far and near to hear the prophet speak [in Dresden, in what was then East Germany]. Some of them traveled several hundred miles. As the hour for the meeting approached, it seemed as if there wasn't room for even one more person. . . .

. . . Sister Margarete Hellmann had suffered an ailment of the hip since youth. As the years came and went, the affliction brought her an ever-increasing burden of pain. Finally, she could walk only with the aid of a pair of crutches. To facilitate her travel from place to place, and to alleviate the terrible pain she keenly felt with every single step, some of the Saints contributed money and bought her a wheelchair. But this relief was short-lived. Soon, even sitting in her wheelchair was accompanied by almost unbearable pain. Then an inflammation of the nerves on the left side of her face further intensified her suffering. One day she heard the heartening news: the prophet of the Lord was to be in Dresden. She had one all-consuming desire—to attend the conference and touch the prophet.

"She had faith and the absolute conviction that the prophet would not even have to take the time to lay his hands upon her head and give her a blessing. She felt assured that it would be with her as it was with a certain woman who, according to St. Mark, had suffered for twelve years and still grew worse. . . .

"Sister Hellman had asked her grandson, Frank, to bring her to the service at an early hour and position her wheelchair near the aisle where the prophet was to pass. This statement from her letter tells the rest of the story in her tender words: 'When our prophet came close to me,' she wrote, 'he warmly shook my hand and looked at me in the spirit of love, as did those who were with him. After that, I did not feel any more pain—not then, nor any to this day. That is the greatest testimony of my life!'" (*Ensign*, November 1978, 36).

To have faith in Jesus Christ is to believe on him and to believe him; to accept as fact what the holy scriptures say about him; to have trust in his divine power; to have confidence in his redemptive capacity; to rely wholly, completely, and only upon *his* merits, mercy, and grace for salvation (2 Nephi 2:8; 31:19; Alma 24:10; Helaman 14:13; Moroni 6:4). For me to have faith in the priesthood is to believe that my ordination is genuine, valid, and as binding in heaven as it is on earth. It is to trust that the priesthood is indeed the power by which God, through his perfect faith, created the worlds and all forms of life on them (Hebrews 11:3). It is to have confidence that when we speak and act as worthy priesthood holders, we are speaking and acting in the place and stead of the Father and the Son. Such knowledge, such understanding, such trust and confidence cannot be generated by mere mortals; it cannot be conjured merely through trying harder. Faith is a gift of the Spirit, an endowment from on high (1 Corinthians 12:9; Ephesians 2:8; Moroni 10:11). Odd, isn't it? God grants us the faith to believe in him and act in his name. Ours is truly a divine investiture of authority.

It was the apostle Paul who taught that "faith cometh by hearing, and hearing by the word of God" (Romans 10:17). "Faith comes by hearing the word of God," Joseph Smith declared, "through the testimony of the servants of God; that testimony is always attended by the Spirit of prophecy and revelation" (*Teachings*, 148). My faith began at my parents' and grandparents' knees, grew in the small Primary classes I attended and was further developed in the Sunday School lessons that were presented, expanded in the testimony meetings where witness was borne month in and month out, and deepened in the zone conferences where my mission presidents and their wives preached the gospel with purity and with power.

My faith has ripened as I have searched the scriptures and thereby heard the word of the Lord (D&C 18:34–36), as well as when I have attended to and taken notes and read and studied the messages of living apostles and prophets over the last forty years. My faith in the priesthood has matured as I have preached the gospel, blessed babies, baptized, confirmed, ordained, set apart, conducted disciplinary councils, cast out devils, healed the sick, and dedicated graves. I know what I know because of what I have experienced firsthand. I have a certain assurance of the power of the priesthood because I have been a repeated recipient of its monumental blessings. And so it is for each of us: With every testimony we bear, every lesson we teach, every opportunity to bless or pass the sacrament we accept, every assignment to participate in the temple we receive, and every time we volunteer to magnify our callings, we thereby stoke the fire that burns within us; we fan the flame of faith. And we thereby increase the impact of our influence.

We exercise faith when we choose Christ and his gospel. We exercise faith when we exercise discipline. We exercise faith when we shun profanity, vulgarity, harshness, crudeness, and spiritual insensitivity. We exercise faith when we refuse to speak unkindly of our fellow Latter-day Saints, when we follow the divine counsel: "Therefore, strengthen your brethren in all your conversation, in all your prayers, in all your exhortations, and in all your doings" (D&C 108:7). We exercise faith when we are faithful—when we demonstrate steadiness, dependability, immovability. "Wherefore, be faithful; stand in the office which I have appointed unto you; succor the weak, lift up the hands which hang down, and strengthen the feeble knees" (D&C 81:5). We exercise faith when in the midst of personal struggle, financial difficulties, unemployment, depression, seasons of unrest or of spiritual aridity, or wanderings of a loved one, we refuse to surrender to circumstances or despair but instead surrender to Jesus— when we do what he has lovingly invited us to do, which is to cast our burdens at his feet and allow him to do the caring, the fretting, the worrying for us (1 Peter 5:7; Matthew

11:28–30). In short, we exercise faith when we take the distant view, when we live today in light of eternity.

When I was working on my master's degree at BYU I was invited by one of my professors, Allen Bergin, to play a game of racquetball late one afternoon. Professor Bergin—now a dear and valued friend—was someone I wanted to get to know better, someone, to be honest, I wanted to impress. I had played a little racquetball through the years and felt confident that a healthy and fit twenty-five year-old could certainly handle an aging college professor!

Well, things didn't turn out exactly as I had anticipated. Allen had me running all over the court while he calmly and efficiently moved from one spot to another and placed the ball exactly where he wanted it (where I wasn't). In the process of running myself to death I heard a horrible sound in my knee, one that was quickly followed by a sharp pain. I had twisted my right knee badly, but I didn't want to seem wimpy and so I kept playing, only now I was bumping into the walls and banging that damaged knee frequently. I later limped back to our small apartment, literally dragging my right leg behind me.

We were only days away from final exams. I knew that I needed to get to a doctor, that my knee would probably require surgery, and that all my hard work through the semester would be jeopardized or at best postponed. As I lay in bed that evening, flinching every time the pain struck, I thought to myself: *What I need is a miracle. I need to be healed. Quickly.*

Soon. Right away! I was not unmindful that not every prayer is answered by God in the affirmative, and not every administration to the sick is followed by an immediate healing. But I felt an uncommon surge of spiritual strength, what I now believe to be an infusion of faith.

The next day I called two of my closest friends, told them of my plight, and said, "I don't have time to have surgery. Neither do I want to throw away almost five months of study. I have a very strong feeling that we need to fast together for a day and have you come to our apartment and give me a blessing." We did fast together, and the next evening my friends arrived at about the same time. One of them anointed my head with oil, and the other sealed the anointing and pronounced a blessing.

That blessing was unlike anything I had ever experienced. My friend called me by name, stated his authority, and then said, quite abruptly, "Brother Robert, we command you to be made whole, beginning this instant. And we also say unto you that your sins are forgiven." He made a few other comments and promises, but my mind was fixated on the initial words. I felt the Spirit of the Lord surge through my body, almost like electricity, from the crown of my head to the soles of my feet. When amen was said, I was filled with the Spirit and overcome with deep emotion. I stood up, embraced both of my dear friends, and learned what I had earlier suspected, namely, that a miracle had indeed been wrought: my knee was completely healed.

Now I suppose there are many in this world who would be eager to explain how it all had happened and to offer some perfectly logical naturalistic explanation. But I know what I know. And I know what I felt and what I experienced. When my buddies left, I dropped to my knees (with no pain) and quickly acknowledged the Source of that satisfying and even sanctifying priesthood power. The Great Physician had heard my cry and had allowed his worthy servants to officiate in his name and by his sacred authority.

"We do not know when the calamities and troubles of the last days will fall upon any of us as individuals or upon bodies of the Saints," declared Elder Bruce R. McConkie. "The Lord deliberately withholds from us the day and hour of his coming and of the tribulations which shall precede it—all as part of the testing and probationary experiences of mortality. He simply tells us to watch and be ready. . . .

"We do not say that all of the Saints will be spared and saved from the coming day of desolation. But we do say there is no promise of safety and no promise of security except for those who love the Lord and who are seeking to do all that he commands.

"It may be, for instance, that *nothing except the power of faith and the authority of the priesthood can save individuals and congregations from the atomic holocausts that surely shall be.*

"And so we raise the warning voice and say: Take heed; prepare; watch and be ready. There is no security in any course except the course of obedience and conformity and righteousness" (*Ensign,* May 1979, 93; emphasis added).

As Mormon wrote to his son Moroni, "Let us labor diligently; for if we should cease to labor, we should be brought under condemnation; for we have a labor to perform whilst in this tabernacle of clay, that we may conquer the enemy of all righteousness, and rest our souls in the kingdom of God" (Moroni 9:6). "After we have done all we could do for the cause of truth," President Joseph F. Smith affirmed, "and withstood the evil that men have brought upon us, and we have been overwhelmed by their wrongs, it is still our duty to stand. *We cannot give up; we must not lie down. Great causes are not won in a single generation. To stand firm in the face of overwhelming opposition, when you have done all you can, is the courage of faith. The courage of faith is the courage of progress*" (*Gospel Doctrine,* 119; emphasis added).

Our Father in heaven will have a faithful people. That faithful people will live on an earth dotted by temples, where miracles and signs and wonders abound and the powers of the priesthood rest upon those holy places in rich abundance. We are preparing for that day right now. Brethren, let us rise up, speak up, speak out, and live worthy of the blood of Jesus Christ, thereby exercising the faith that leads to life and salvation.

POINTS TO PONDER

1. Have I prayed earnestly for the gift of faith?
2. What are some ways I can tell my faith is maturing?

3. Joseph Smith taught that we work by faith when we work by the power of "mental exertion instead of physical force" (*Lectures on Faith*, 7:3). What mental exertion do I need to undertake to operate by faith?

4. A significant part of being a man of faith is being a faithful man. What can I do to demonstrate my faithfulness?

ETERNAL PRIESTHOOD POWER
AND INFLUENCE

IT HAS BEEN MY CONSUMMATE privilege to sit at the feet of noble priesthood holders, to be schooled and tutored by men of God who love the Lord and represent him with dignity and fidelity. The men to whom I refer possess a quiet confidence that bespeaks an unconditional surrender and trust in the will and purposes of our God. They proceed along the path of faith, always and ever aware that they walk in the shadow of their Master. They are not perfect, but they are centered. They are not necessarily brilliant, but they are wise as to the things of holiness. They are not necessarily charismatic in the world's way of measuring things, but their lives are in fact Spirit-breathed and their actions Spirit-directed. They are dynamic in their enthusiasm for truth and goodness, yet settled and grounded in the faith, never "moved away from the hope of the gospel" (Colossians 1:23). They are men of the Holy Priesthood, men of Christ, men of remarkable influence. Their eye is single to his glory, and thus their bodies are filled with his light; they comprehend things that are unreachable and unfathomable to men and women of the world (D&C 88:67). They walk with the Lord.

Our God is all-powerful and can transform weakness into strength and turn frailty and infirmity into dynamic discipleship, just as he did with Enoch of old (Moses 6:31–34; 7:13). And so I suppose that every time you or I should feel incapable, inadequate, and out of our league when we are called to move the mountains within our spiritual purview, it would be worthwhile to think of our good friend and scriptural prototype, Enoch: poor old, stammering, stuttering Enoch, a man whom we now identify with transcendent righteousness and the ultimate mortal attainment (Moses 7:18, 69).

While writing this passage, I couldn't help but think of the beautiful Protestant hymn I learned in my teenage years, one our ward choir sang more than once:

> I come to the garden alone,
> While the dew is still on the roses,
> And the voice I hear,
> Falling on my ear,
> The Son of God discloses.
>
> He speaks, and the sound of His voice
> Is so sweet the birds hush their singing,
> And the melody
> That He gave to me,
> Within my heart is ringing.

Chorus:
And He walks with me,
And He talks with me,
And He tells me I am His own;
And the joy we share
As we tarry there,
None other has ever known.
(*Cokesbury Worship Hymnal,* no. 62)

A priesthood holder walks with the Lord when he seeks to emulate his Lord, to do what Jesus would do. In addition, a priesthood holder walks with the Lord—

- When he grasps and inculcates the supernal truth that salvation comes by the merits and mercy and grace of the Holy Messiah (2 Nephi 2:8; 31:19; Moroni 6:4).

- When he chooses not to walk with the world but rather to take the road less traveled.

- When he leads his family in daily prayer, weekly family home evening, and regular and consistent church attendance.

- When he treats his wife as a queen, treats his children with patience and respect, and creates a home environment that is safe, secure, and serene, a home that becomes, by the power of the Holy Ghost, a little bit of heaven on earth.

- When he walks in the light of the Spirit and thereby enjoys fellowship with the Father and the Son (1 John 1:7).

- When he charts a course to eternal life, makes and is true to the covenants of salvation, stays in the mainstream of the Church, and dies in the faith, thereby making his calling and election to eternal life certain and sure (see McConkie, funeral address, 5).

One Sunday morning we finished our bishopric meeting and welcomed the priesthood leaders into the office to begin the priesthood executive committee meeting. I noticed a scowl on the face of the high priest group leader, something rather uncommon for such a light-hearted and happy man. I asked privately, "What's wrong?"

He shook his head and said, "Nothing. I'm okay."

He made very few comments during the meeting (which was unusual), and what he did say was accompanied by an air of bitterness.

I stayed out of his way throughout the three-hour block of meetings and waited until priesthood meeting was over. Then I walked with him to his car and pursued again, "Come on, Larry, what's up? Talk to me about it."

Larry heaved a huge sigh and replied, "Bishop, you know that last night was our annual high priest group social, don't you?"

I responded hesitantly that I did know that and was sorry

I had been unable to be there—assuming that perhaps that was why he was so upset.

"No, no," Larry said. "I know you have a million things to do, and we didn't anticipate that you would make it. But I am very disturbed that a couple of people in the group didn't show. For example, Brother Watson didn't come. He has missed two in a row now. What bothers me the most is that I found out why he wasn't there."

I asked what Larry had learned.

"He decided to take his family bowling instead. That's why. Man, does that tick me off!"

I probably displayed my feelings (I usually do), but I said, "Bowling with his family, huh? That is serious. Perhaps I ought to ask him not to take the sacrament for a month or, depending on his attitude, summon him into a disciplinary council. We just cannot permit this kind of blatant sin to continue!"

Larry looked sternly into my eyes and asked, "Are you making fun of me?"

I said, "I suppose I am. I know you want to have a good turnout to your activities and that it builds group brotherhood, but, my goodness, the man spent the evening with his family. Let's don't forget why we're doing what we're doing. Everything we do in this Church is done to bless individuals and strengthen families."

I was pleased when a tiny smile crept onto Larry's face, and he answered, "Yeah, I guess I'm acting a little silly, huh?"

We must avoid or withstand the temptation to confuse means with ends. The Church is a godsend, an inspired program established to unify and perfect the Saints and to empower us to remain orthodox in doctrine and practice (Ephesians 4:11–14), but it is scaffolding used to assist in the construction of a glorious temple, namely, the eternal family unit.

So here we are—deacons and teachers and priests and elders and high priests—each called to divine service and ordained to glory. Our task is not to lead the whole Church, for that is the calling of our beloved prophet-leader and his associates, the counselors in the First Presidency and the Quorum of the Twelve Apostles. Our task is not so much to move Mount Zerin, as did the brother of Jared (Ether 12:30), as it is to overcome spiritual inertia and allow our Master to transform our half-hearted obedience into dynamic discipleship. Our duty is not necessarily to raise the dead so much as it is to be born again, to put to death the old man of sin and put on Christ, thereby becoming new creatures of the Holy Ghost. Our duty may not be to command and still the threatening waves of the Sea of Galilee as it is to shore up the faithless and to calm and console the troubled hearts of the lonely, the disabled, and the disconsolate.

Our assignment as individuals may not be to lead a coliseum full of converted persons to the waters of baptism so much as it is to serve as true undershepherds to a few who have wandered from the fold. Our assignment may not be to speak with a voice of thunder to shake the earth and declare repentance to every nation, kindred, tongue, and people but rather to receive with gospel gladness the sacred charge to bear witness in word and deed of the message of salvation to those who reside within our own tiny worlds of influence. To be sure, those who magnify their callings and are steadfast in the faith are entitled to the grand accolade: "Well done, thou good and faithful servant: thou hast been faithful over a few things, I will make thee ruler over many things: enter thou into the joy of thy Lord" (Matthew 25:21).

We have been promised in modern revelation that if we are true to priesthood principles in how we live and lead, "the doctrine of the priesthood shall distil upon [our] soul[s] as the dews from heaven" (D&C 121:45). Elder Bruce R. McConkie pulled back the curtains of heaven and implored:

"My brethren of the priesthood: To all of you, to all holders of the Aaronic and Melchizedek Priesthoods, I issue this challenge: Come, learn the doctrine of the priesthood; come, live as befits one who is a servant of the Lord.

"This doctrine, this doctrine of the priesthood—unknown in the world and but little known even in the Church—cannot be learned out of the scriptures alone. It is not set forth in the sermons and teachings of the prophets and Apostles, except in small measure.

"The doctrine of the priesthood is known only by personal revelation. It comes, line upon line and precept upon precept, by the power of the Holy Ghost to those who love and serve God with all their heart, might, mind, and strength (see D&C 98:12). . . .

"Priesthood is power like none other on earth or in heaven. It is the very power of God himself, the power by which the worlds were made, the power by which all things are regulated, upheld, and preserved.

"It is the power of faith, the faith by which the Father creates and governs. God is God because he is the embodiment of all faith and all power and all priesthood. The life he lives is named eternal life.

"And the extent to which we become like him is the extent to which we gain his faith, acquire his power, and exercise his priesthood. And when we have become like him in the full and true sense, then we also shall have eternal life.

"Faith and priesthood go hand in hand. Faith is power and power is priesthood. . . .

"As the Lord lives, [the priesthood] is his holy order, and all those priesthood holders of every nation and kindred and tongue and people and race and color who will keep the covenant shall abide as priests forever, ruling and reigning everlastingly with the great High Priest of our profession, who is the Lord Jesus Christ. . . .

"What, then, is the doctrine of the priesthood? And how shall we live as the servants of the Lord? . . .

"It is that we have power, by faith, to govern and control all things, both temporal and spiritual; to work miracles and perfect lives; to stand in the presence of God and be like him because we have gained his faith, his perfections, and his power, or in other words the fulness of his priesthood. . . .

"Truly, there is power in the priesthood—power to do all things! . . .

"Truly there is power in the priesthood—a power which we seek to acquire to use, a power which we devoutly pray may rest upon us and upon our posterity forever" (*Ensign*, May 1982, 32–34).

I close with a note of soberness and of witness. There is tremendous power in the influence of a righteous man. As we learned from Gideon of old, that ancient man of valor and influence, with the Lord on our side we are always in the majority and are prepared thereby for victory (Judges 6–8). We live in a time of earth's history wherein there is a burgeoning polarization. Satan and his forces are combined (D&C 38:12) and constitute a formidable enemy to the Righteous One and the soldiers within his ranks. At the same time, perhaps there has seldom been a generation of Saints who were more steeped in the language and logic and learning of holy scripture and who have chosen freely to give their all, including their wills, in sacrifice and pure consecration. Never before have the temptations and taunts from the spacious building been more blatant or subtle as they are now, so sophisticated and malevolent as to almost deceive the very elect according to the covenant (Joseph Smith-Matthew 1:22). And yet never before has the Spirit of the Lord been poured out upon all flesh (Joel 2:28) with such intensity as right now, resulting not only in a mass conversion to the faith of Jesus Christ but also in technological advances and scientific developments that make the spread of the sacred word to all lands much more doable.

I know that God our Heavenly Father lives, that he is the Father of our spirits (Numbers 16:22; 27:16; Hebrews 12:9), that he has a body of flesh and bones as tangible as man's (D&C 130:22), and that we are created in his image and likeness. Jesus Christ is his Only Begotten Son in the flesh and is our Savior, our Lord, our God, the great apostle and High Priest of our profession (Hebrews 3:1) and our Only Hope for redemption from death and hell and endless torment. I testify that salvation comes by and through his holy name (Acts 4:12; Mosiah 3:17) and through his merits and mercy and grace (2 Nephi 2:8; 31:19; Moroni 6:4) and in no other way.

The same Spirit that confirms to my soul the living reality and saving verity of the Godhead bears a like witness of the restored gospel—that Joseph Smith was called and prepared to stand as a modern prophet and the head of the dispensation of the fulness of times (Ephesians 1:10; D&C 128:18); that angels have been sent from on high to bestow priesthood authority and keys, the same keys that were conferred upon Peter, James, and John anciently (John 15:16; D&C 27:12–13; 112:30–32), the keys that bind on earth and seal in heaven (Matthew 16:19; 18:18; D&C 128:9–11); that doctrinal revelation and institutional direction have come from the Almighty, as well as additional books of holy scripture, each making its own distinctive contribution but bearing a united testimony of the Savior, including the essential truthfulness of the Bible (1 Nephi 13:39–40); and that the keys of the kingdom of God have come down to our time in rightful succession, so that the president of The Church of Jesus Christ of Latter-day Saints holds and exercises all of those keys in their fulness.

Without question, there is goodness and truth and spiritual strength to be found among men and women throughout the earth. I bear solemn witness, however, that the Holy Priesthood, after the Order of the Son of God—what we as Latter-day Saints call the Melchizedek Priesthood—is not limited to Jesus alone, as many in the Christian world attest, but is available to those called by prophecy and revelation and is conferred by the laying on of hands (Articles of Faith 1:5; also D&C 1:20). The priesthood is neither myth nor metaphor. It is real. It is necessary for the performance of the saving ordinances (sacraments), each of which is an extension and a part of that package we know as faith in the Lord Jesus Christ. It is the greatest power in time and in eternity.

Men of influence, men of power, have never been needed more than they are during this generation. Children, both boys and girls, deserve to have a kindly and honorable priesthood holder at the head of their family. Wives and mothers are entitled to live together in love with a man whose heart is pure, whose life is unblemished, whose language is unsullied, whose lips utter no guile, a man whose presence and prayers bring down blessings from heaven. And our communities are in desperate need of men of faith, men who will speak up for morality, decency, God-ordained marriage between one man and one woman, the traditional family unit, and absolute values. We must respond courageously to the call that has come to each of us, for we have a date with destiny. We have a world to prepare for the coming of its Rightful Ruler, the King of kings and Lord of lords, even Christ Jesus our Redeemer.

I am thrilled to live when I do. This is a day of consummate opportunity and unlimited promise. I am excited to be a member of what may well be the largest body of priesthood holders in the history of the world. And these men and boys are not only numerous but noble; not only kind but capable; not only fearless but faithful; and not only heroic but holy. No one of us is perfect, but God's army is as spiritual as it is spread out.

We are surely a part of the prophetic vision had by Nephi, son of Lehi: "And it came to pass that I, Nephi, beheld the power of the Lamb of God, that it descended upon the saints of the church of the Lamb, and upon the covenant people of the Lord, who were scattered upon all the face of the earth; and they were armed with righteousness and with the power of God in great glory" (1 Nephi 14:14; compare Revelation 17:14).

Invested with that kind of power, we cannot fail. Dressed in the robes of righteousness and looking only to our Leader for divine direction, we will become a part of God's grand success story. This earth, cleansed and sanctified, will become heaven. Eternal life, exaltation on this celestial planet, will then be ours, and eternal families will dwell here everlastingly in the presence of God the Father and his Son Jesus Christ. Truly, as William W. Phelps wrote under inspiration, "There is no end to priesthood" (*Hymns*, no. 284).

POINTS TO PONDER

1. If the only way I demonstrate power in the priesthood is through blessing the sick, what will I do in the Millennium? What are some other ways to demonstrate this power in my home and among the other children of God?

2. We are told that "this same Priesthood, which was in the beginning, shall be in the end of the world also" (Moses 6:7). What am I doing to develop into a righteous, God-fearing, Spirit-led patriarch, working harmoniously with my wife in leading my family?

3. How can I draw upon the powers of the priesthood in standing boldly against the growing tide of immorality and secularism in our world?

4. The extent of priesthood power we will enjoy in eternity is inextricably tied to the priesthood power and influence we enjoy in time. Given where I am now, what can I anticipate in eternity?

REFERENCES

Andrus, Hyrum L., and Helen Mae Andrus. *They Knew the Prophet.* Salt Lake City: Bookcraft, 1974.

Bednar, David A. "Pray Always." *Ensign,* November 2008, 41–44.

Benson, Ezra Taft. "Beware of Pride." *Ensign,* May 1989, 4–7.

Clark, J. Reuben Jr. In Conference Report, April 1951, 154.

The Cokesbury Worship Hymnal. Edited by C. A. Bowen. New York: Abingdon-Cokesbury Press, n.d.

Eyring, Henry B. "O Remember, Remember." *Ensign,* November 2007, 67–69.

Hafen, Bruce C. *The Broken Heart: Applying the Atonement to Life's Experiences.* Salt Lake City: Deseret Book, 1989.

Hales, Robert D. "Holy Scriptures: The Power of God unto Our Salvation." *Ensign,* November 2006, 24–27.

Hinckley, Gordon B. "Find the Lambs, Feed the Sheep." *Ensign,* May 1999, 104–10.

Holland, Jeffrey R. "The Atonement of Jesus Christ." *Ensign,* March 2008, 32–38.

——. "Witnesses unto Me." *Ensign,* May 2001, 14–16.

Hunter, Howard W. "Hallowed Be Thy Name." *Ensign,* November 1977, 52–54.

——. "'Jesus, the Very Thought of Thee.'" *Ensign,* May 1993, 63–65.

——. *That We Might Have Joy.* Salt Lake City: Deseret Book, 1994.

Hymns of The Church of Jesus Christ of Latter-day Saints. Salt Lake City: The Church of Jesus Christ of Latter-day Saints, 1985.

Journal of Discourses. 26 vols. Liverpool: F. D. Richards & Sons, 1851–86.

Lee, Harold B. "A Blessing for the Saints." *Ensign,* January 1973, 133–34.

——. "Understanding Who We Are Brings Self-Respect." *Ensign,* January 1974, 2–6.

Lewis, C. S. *Mere Christianity.* New York: Touchstone, 1996.

Maxwell, Neal A. *Plain and Precious Things.* Salt Lake City: Deseret Book, 1983.

——. "What Should We Pray For?" In *Prayer.* Salt Lake City: Deseret Book, 1978.

——. "Why Not Now?" *Ensign,* November 1974, 12–13.

McConkie, Bruce R. Address at the funeral of S. Dilworth Young, transcript, 13 July 1981.

——. *Doctrines of the Restoration: Sermons & Writings of Bruce R. McConkie.* Edited by Mark L. McConkie. Salt Lake City: Bookcraft, 1989.

——. "The Doctrine of the Priesthood." *Ensign,* May 1982, 32–34.

——. *Let Every Man Learn His Duty: The Ten Commandments of Priesthood Correlation and the Home Teaching Constitution.* Salt Lake City: Deseret Book, 1976.

——. "Why the Lord Ordained Prayer." In *Prayer.* Salt Lake City: Deseret Book, 1978.

——. "Stand Independent above All Other Creatures." *Ensign,* May 1979, 92–94.

Monson, Thomas S. "Examples of Righteousness." *Ensign,* May 2008, 65–68.

——. "A Royal Priesthood." *Ensign,* November 2007, 59–61.

——. "The Way of the Master." *Ensign,* January 2003, 4–7.

——. "Welcome to Conference." *Ensign,* November 2008, 4–6.

The New Shorter Oxford English Dictionary, 2 vols. Edited by Lesley Brown. Oxford: Clarendon Press, 1993.

Oaks, Dallin H. *The Lord's Way.* Salt Lake City: Deseret Book, 1991.

Packer, Boyd K. "The Bishop and His Counselors." *Ensign,* May 1999, 57–64.

——. "Covenants." *Ensign,* May 1987, 22–25.

——. "The Mediator." *Ensign,* May 1977, 54–56.

Pratt, Parley P. *Key to the Science of Theology.* Salt Lake City: Deseret Book, 1978.

Roberts, B. H. *The Gospel and Man's Relationship to Deity.* Salt Lake City: Deseret Book, 1966.

Smith, Joseph. *History of The Church of Jesus Christ of Latter-day Saints.* Edited by B. H. Roberts. 2d ed. rev. 7 vols. Salt Lake City: Deseret Book, 1957.

———. *Lectures on Faith*. Salt Lake City: Deseret Book, 1985.

———. *Teachings of the Prophet Joseph Smith*. Selected by Joseph Fielding Smith. Salt Lake City: Deseret Book, 1976.

Smith, Joseph F. *Gospel Doctrine*. Salt Lake City: Deseret Book, 1971.

Smith, Joseph Fielding. Conference Report, April 1969, 121, 123.

Tanner, N. Eldon. "No Greater Honor: The Woman's Role." *Ensign*, January 1974, 7–10.

Uchtdorf, Dieter F. "Lift Where You Stand." *Ensign*, November 2008, 53–56.

Webster, Noah. *American Dictionary of the English Language*. 1828. Reprint, San Francisco: Foundation for American Christian Education, 1980.

Wickman, Lance B. "Today." *Ensign*, May 2008, 103–5.

Woodruff, Wilford. *Discourses of Wilford Woodruff*. Edited by G. Homer Durham. Salt Lake City: Bookcraft, 1969.

Wright, N. T. *The Last Word: Beyond the Bible Wars to a New Understanding of the Authority of Scripture*. New York: Harper, 2005.

Wirthlin, Joseph B. "Let Your Light So Shine." *Ensign*, November 1978, 36–37.

INDEX

California, 114–16
Calling(s): being chosen and, 25–26;
    aspiring to, 28–30; acquitting
    ourselves and, 55–60; pride in,
    86–87
Celestial kingdom, Joseph Smith
    on humility and, 54–55
Change: Thomas S. Monson on, 9;
    Holy Ghost and, 47–48;
    procrastinating, 65–68
Chapple, Richard, 55
Children, becoming like, 50–55
Children of God, recognizing
    identity as, 7–8
Choices, making, 120–22
Chosen, 25–26
Church of Jesus Christ of Latter-
    day Saints: bearing witness of
    truthfulness of, 12; improving
    people's perceptions of, 14–15;
    growth of, 18; three internal
    threats to, 34; young man wants
    to leave, 57–60; proving
    truthfulness of, 106–7; Holy
    Ghost as evidence of
    truthfulness of, 116–17; family
    as central part of, 139–41;
    author's testimony of, 145–46
Clark, J. Reuben Jr., 29
Coconut cream pie, 44–45
Cokesbury Worship Hymnal,
    137–38
Commandments: keeping, 4–6;
    acting on, 25–26
Compliments, 86–87
Courage of faith, 134
Covenants, 8–9
Covetousness, 30–32

Dead Sea Scrolls, 106–7
Death, of premature baby, 109–12
Decisions, making, 120–22
Dependence, of children, 51
Distraction, 93
Divine worth, 7–8
Dixon, Charles, 1–2
Dobson, James, 37–38
Duplicity, 93–94

Evans, Richard L., 27
Eyring, Henry B., 88

Faith: in Jesus Christ, 42, 128–29;
    transferring, 125–28;
    strengthening, 129–30;
    exercising, 130–33; preparing for
    Second Coming and, 133–34;
    courage of, 134
Family, importance of, 139–41
Fatigue, 94–95
First Vision, 21–22
Florida State University, 15–18,
    45–46
Foreordination, 2–3, 25, 32–33
Forgiveness, of children, 52

General Handbook of Instructions,
    55–56
God: understanding, through
    priesthood, x; recognizing
    identity as child of, 7–8;
    standing as witnesses of, 11–13;
    preparing to meet, 65–70;
    Joseph Smith on love of, 88–89;
    drawing closer to, 91–92;
    communicating with, 92; Joseph
    Smith on communing with, 102;

ABOUT THE AUTHOR

Robert L. Millet is an Abraham O. Smoot University Professor, professor of ancient scripture, and former dean of Religious Education at Brigham Young University. He received his bachelor's and master's degrees at BYU in psychology and his Ph.D. from Florida State University in religious studies. He has served in The Church of Jesus Christ of Latter-day Saints as a bishop, a stake president, and a member of the Materials Evaluation Committee. During the past twelve years, much of his professional time has been spent in interfaith relations in an effort to build bridges of understanding and friendship between members of the Church and those of other faiths.

A well-beloved speaker who is much in demand, Brother Millet is the author of numerous books, including *Men of Valor, Holding Fast, Are We There Yet? Grace Works,* and *When a Child Wanders.* He is also the coauthor, with Lloyd D. Newell, of a series of daily devotional books: *Jesus, the Very Thought of*

Thee; When Ye Shall Receive These Things; Draw Near unto Me; and *A Lamp unto My Feet.*

Brother Millet and his wife, Shauna, are the parents of six children and reside in Orem, Utah.